The
International
Monetary
Tangle

CT/UB/£7.85.

The International Monetary Tangle

Myths and Realities

By *Guillaume Guindey*

Translated by Michael L. Hoffman

Basil Blackwell · Oxford

Contents

The
International
Monetary
Tangle

To the Memory of
William M. Tomlinson
United States Treasury Representative
1918-1955

Preface

What do the international monetary issues with which the world has been grappling for more than ten years really consist of? To what extent do they arise from the application of erroneous concepts? To what extent are the troubles due, rather, to mistakes in management? The Bretton Woods system has been largely abandoned since 1971 and a new regime has replaced it. Can we now form an opinion about this regime? Can it — and under what conditions — provide an acceptable solution? Is it bound to be based on the dollar? What will be the future of gold? What will be the future of that new international fiduciary money baptized Special Drawing Rights which was created in 1968? All these questions, and others of the same nature, have been the object of widespread debate for several years. Opposing viewpoints have been defended by equally distinguished and respectable intellects. All the various theses have been supported and all the arguments brought forward.

In the following pages we will approach these problems by a path that has been little explored up to now. We will approach them from the historical angle. A new epoch in international monetary relations began just over thirty years ago, with the establishment of the International Monetary Fund. A natural approach is to recall the phases through which it has passed, and the difficulties with which it has met, and to reflect on this evolution. Such an enterprise, though it may not supply answers to all the questions, will highlight certain features. It should cause many issues to be seen in an instructive light.

The first part of the present essay is, therefore, devoted to the principal stages and vicissitudes of international monetary cooperation since the end of World War II. The lessons to be drawn from this historical review form the object of the second part.

Part One

A LOOK AT THIRTY-THREE YEARS
OF INTERNATIONAL MONETARY COOPERATION

International monetary cooperation was born well before World War II. Important initiatives were taken between the great wars of 1914-18 and 1939-45. But a new era, which is ours, began with the conclusion of the Bretton Woods agreements. As active preparations for the Bretton Woods Conference began in 1943, we may say that this new era began thirty-three years ago.

In the course of these thirty-three years, the year 1958 marks a first turning point, for two reasons. First, it was in 1958 that the balance of payments of the United States entered a long period of deficits, and that the dogma of the equivalence of the dollar and gold began to be openly questioned. Second, it was in 1958 that the decision was made to reestablish the convertibility of the principal European currencies and that the European Payments Union, which since 1950 had provided an important instrument of monetary collaboration among the countries of Western Europe, was dissolved.

The second turning point was clearly the abandonment, in 1971, of the convertibility of the dollar and the profound changes that this entailed.

We must therefore consider as separate periods the one that ended in 1958, the one from 1958 to 1971, and the one that began in 1971.

CHAPTER I

The Bretton Woods Charter

The men who prepared and brought to fruition the Bretton Woods Conference — in the middle of a war — worked under the influence of their experience and their memories. Having witnessed the disorders of the pre-1939 period, they felt the need to endow the world with a monetary order. Deeply conscious of the errors committed between the two wars, they sought to avoid a repetition. They were not engaged in a theoretical exercise.

One of their beliefs was that it was of the highest importance to guarantee the freedom of current payments, particularly commercial payments. It was essential to avoid quotas or other quantitative controls that would place limits on the volume of merchandise trade. Exchange controls that restrict normal settlements between one country and another should be avoided. So should clearing agreements or other similar arrangements based on the notion that bilateral balances should be enforced — devices that end up by paralyzing competition and establishing discrimination. It was, in their view, indispensable that current payments should not only be free of all restrictions but also be settled in currencies usable anywhere in the world. And it would be desirable that all members of the international community enter into engagements covering these various matters.

Engagements of such a nature are, however, bound to remain inadequate if not accompanied by discipline in matters of exchange rate policy. A country may always be tempted to improve its competitive position by an excessive depreciation of its currency, which is likely to force its neighbors to take protective measures. Prewar experience demonstrated that there are ingenious techniques, involving multiple exchange rates, through which particular countries can obtain undue advantages. These also are likely to lead to countermeasures. It was therefore necessary that there be surveillance. Its object would be to see that each currency had a realistic parity and, at the same time, to avoid unwarranted changes in exchange rates.

Another conviction of the men of Bretton Woods concerned the need for a system of mutual support to aid countries in balance of payments difficulties. A deficit country needs time — often two or three years — to adopt a corrective program and carry it out. If the country has no exchange resources during this period except its own reserves, it may have to take extreme measures of self-defense (e.g., excessive devaluation, exchange and import restrictions) likely both to compromise its own recovery and to harm the rest of the international community. It is in the general interest that such a country be given credit. This truth became apparent between the two wars. Credits to nations in difficulty took the form of international loans floated in the market or of government-to-government loans. But such operations had to be carried out case by case, often slowly and against many obstacles. One of the original features of the Bretton Woods agreements was the establishment in advance among the signatories of a multilateral mechanism for the reciprocal granting of credits, thanks to which in case of need each could quickly borrow from all, and each could quickly lend to all. To obtain such credits the borrowing country would naturally have to put into effect an adequate corrective program.

To attain all these objectives, an international organism for monetary cooperation was indispensable. It would have a triple function. It must assure that the countries respect their undertakings concerning the freedom and multilateralization of current payments. It must exercise surveillance over national decisions to devalue. It must operate a collective Fund on which, within definite limits, each country could draw in case of need and which, within certain limits, could replenish itself by calling on the contributions of each member country. Thus the founders were led to the conception of the International Monetary Fund and to the principle that a quota should be assigned to each member. This institution would ideally be worldwide, since the purpose was to establish a monetary order that would permit the growth of commerce of all nations with all nations.[1]

Logically, the International Monetary Fund had to assume a fourth function. During the great crisis of the 1930s, experience had shown that the fixing of the price of gold and decisions to raise or not to raise that price could have a large influence on the state of the whole world economy. Decisions having such important effects could not be left to the authorities of one country, or of only a few countries, no matter how important they might be. Moreover, this was a matter affecting the value of all existing monetary reserves and influencing the volume of production of new gold. It stood to reason that such decisions should be made in the future within the framework of the International Monetary Fund, in the form of collective resolutions of its members.

The men of Bretton Woods had not merely the merit of defining clearly a number of objectives. They also had the merit of understanding that in practice it was essential to retain great flexibility.

Consider the freedom and multilateralization of current payments. The Bretton Woods agreements were destined to take effect in a world fenced in by exchange controls and a network

---

1. As matters turned out, Switzerland remained apart, while the USSR, after participating in the Bretton Woods Conference, refused to adhere to the agreements. And the other Communist countries of Eastern Europe, except Yugoslavia, abstained or withdrew. If the USSR had joined, the relative weight of the U.S. quota in the IMF would have been reduced.

of clearing and payments agreements, the heritages of the prewar and wartime periods. It would take some time and effort
to get rid of exchange controls (at least to narrow their field
to controls on capital movements) and to get away from bilateralism by establishing convertibility. Even when these results had been generally achieved, it was only to be expected
that some country would backslide. The drafters of the charter
had the wisdom to provide for a period of transition and for the
later possibility of temporary derogations.

Consider the rules concerning changes in parities. As far as
possible, countries facing balance of payments difficulties
should be allowed to make their own choices among different
methods of correcting their situations. In particular, they
should be allowed to choose between a policy of devaluing and
a policy of defending the parities of their currencies without a
devaluation by means of appropriate internal measures. The
Bretton Woods charter prudently abstained from laying down a
rigid doctrine on this subject; each country retains responsibility for initiating a change in the parity of its currency. The
International Monetary Fund was not granted the initiative with
respect to changes in parities. It was, on the other hand, given
the task of pronouncing judgment on proposals for parity
changes that might be submitted to it. It was also given the
task — which could lead very far — of pronouncing on the legitimacy of restrictive practices that might be the consequence
of a policy of nondevaluation. Thus the charter retained great
flexibility, which enabled the Fund to adapt to different kinds
of situations without affronting national sovereignty. Finally,
in this connection it was stipulated that changes involving a
modification of less than ten percent of the initial parity of a
currency would be approved by the Fund without question.

In a general way, the founders of the Fund believed that it
could exercise the authority given to it only if it was prepared
to evaluate particular cases in the light of the situation in each
country at any given moment. Consequently, at the same time
that they defined general objectives, they foresaw that when a
delicate problem came up affecting a member country (whether

The Bretton Woods Charter

it was a parity change or the application of restrictive measures forbidden by the Articles), the Fund must have at hand
sufficient information about the country to enable it to form a
judgment in the light of all the relevant facts. The Fund could
carry out its task only if it followed in a continuing fashion the
economic and financial evolution of each of its member countries.

Remarkable as it was, the work of the Bretton Woods Conference inevitably could not solve all questions.

One delicate problem was that of long- or medium-term
credits that many countries were going to need. The European
nations, devastated and impoverished by the war, would temporarily need exceptional assistance the principal source of which
would have to be North America. The developing nations would
need financial assistance from the industrial states for many
years. Finally, it had been learned between the two wars that
countries struggling with monetary difficulties would sometimes need "stabilization credits" of more or less long term
in order to reconstitute their reserves.

The drafters of the charter understood that it would be hope-
less to try to establish a monetary order if these problems
were not resolved. They also understood that the solutions
could not be of a monetary nature, that they could not be provided by the Fund, and that they would involve the setting up of
new mechanisms capable of attracting public and private sav-
ings. It was in the light of these considerations that they created, along with the Fund, the International Bank for Reconstruction and Development (the World Bank), an institution
which although of a nonmonetary character, provided an indispensable complement to the Fund.

In the eyes of the founders, the establishment of the Bank
represented only a partial solution to the problem of medium-
and long-term credit. The American government, in particular,
did not rule out the possibility of granting bilateral assistance
to the countries of Europe, Japan, and the developing countries.
The men of Bretton Woods nevertheless harbored some illusions

9

as to the extent of the services that could be expected from the
World Bank. They thought that it could play an important role
in the reconstruction of the industrial areas ruined by the war;
they thought that it might even grant "stabilization loans" to
complement the assistance available from the Monetary Fund.
As we now know, the World Bank very soon had to limit its
activities to development assistance, in which field it has rendered eminent service. The Bretton Woods Conference had in
fact, therefore, left it up to mechanisms other than those it
created to carry out the large international financial operations
required to bring about world economic stability. This was, indeed, probably the only possible line of conduct. But it had the
effect of leaving it uncertain whether, and how, the required
tasks would be carried out.

Another related question left in a somewhat equivocal state
was that of international capital movements and the disturbances they can create in balances of payments.

The Bretton Woods charter, which was very precise concerning transfers arising out of current operations (commercial or
financial), treated capital movements very tentatively. In fact
the Articles were based entirely on a distinction between the
two categories of transactions and on the idea that the priority
objectives were freedom for current payments and the covering
of deficits arising from current operations. The Articles permitted a resort to exchange controls as applied to capital movements; they even foresaw that, under certain circumstances,
the Fund might recommend such action. The United States, in
fact, made Congressional ratification of the agreements conditional on an interpretation of the Fund Articles that would prevent use of Fund resources to finance "significant and prolonged outflows of capital."

How could deficits arising from capital exports be handled?
Could exchange controls eliminate such deficits? Once it was
accepted that the Fund should be discouraged from allowing its
limited resources to be substantially diverted from their fundamental objective in order to cover capital movements, would it
not be desirable to find other methods for equilibrating the cap-

ital element in balances of payments? What methods could there be? Would it not be necessary to organize compensatory credit operations? In what form and in what framework could they best be arranged? The drafters of the Bretton Woods charter trusted in the future to bring answers to these questions.

They also left a third problem somewhat in the shade: that of "extreme creditors," countries whose balance of payments surpluses, because of their importance and their durable character, threaten to create difficulties for the rest of the international community. True, they did not ignore this matter. While considering that countries in deficit should always be able to reestablish equilibrium in their external accounts through appropriate policies, the drafters of the charter believed that the "extreme creditors" also had some obligations. That is why they confronted "extreme creditors" with the formidable threat inherent in the power granted to the Fund to declare that a currency is "scarce" within the meaning of the Articles, thereby making it legal to apply discriminatory restrictions on current payments to the country in question. What concessions could an "extreme creditor" make to avoid such an extremity? The Articles do not say precisely, although they do envisage the eventuality of loans to the Fund by a member country. Experience has shown that recourse to the "scarce currency" clause is regarded as such a drastic sanction that it has never been applied. "Extreme creditor" countries have preferred to provide extensive financial facilities rather than risk having the clause applied to them. The upshot is that the Articles, while recognizing the principle that "extreme creditors" have some obligations, remain somewhat foggy as to their nature.

The charter is also vague on another delicate subject. What place in the new system would remain for agreements for monetary cooperation between two countries, or among a small number of countries, and how would such agreements be reconciled with the Fund's operations?

It appears that there was no question, in the thinking of the drafters, of excluding the possibility of agreements of that nature, but they felt that it would be wise to see to it that their contents conformed to the purposes of the Fund. In fact, as early as December 1945 the United States and Great Britain, the two principal promoters of the charter, made a bilateral agreement which provided, in the context of an American loan, for important changes in the status of the pound sterling. Furthermore, there was no suggestion at Bretton Woods that multilateral arrangements among a limited number of countries, such as those of the sterling area, should be proscribed. And no stipulation in the Articles conferred on the Fund a monopoly in the field of international monetary cooperation.

This problem, however, was not faced squarely at Bretton Woods. If it had been, the conference doubtless would not have decided — as it did — to liquidate the Bank for International Settlements. That institution, established in 1930, had, among other functions, the task of promoting cooperation among central banks; its membership included most of the principal European central banks as well as the American banking system. Even though it had been forced into a state of somnolence during the war, the BIS still existed in 1944. Among various operations it had carried out during the war were some gold purchases, which led the American Treasury to believe, quite wrongly, that it had agreed to aid Hitler's Germany dispose of stolen metal. This suspicion would have warranted nothing more than an investigation if it had been thought otherwise desirable to maintain an instrument for cooperation among European central banks such as the BIS. Neither the Americans nor the British thought so, and the other participants accepted their view.

Thus the men of Bretton Woods were not entirely free of the illusion that the establishment of the Fund would suffice to settle nearly all problems in international monetary cooperation. From this angle the Anglo-American agreement of December 1945 was an exception, justified by the need for a special degree of collaboration between the two countries of greatest monetary importance; the only two whose monies were reserve currencies; the only two in which there were then large financial markets. It is clear that it was the intention of the United States and Great Britain to establish an Anglo-American predominance in monetary affairs which, in American eyes, was destined to become more American than British. There was clearly a risk of misunderstanding as to what place would remain for subsequent monetary cooperation among a limited group of countries, more particularly for European or Western monetary cooperation.

A final uncertainty concerned the weight to be given to the engagements contracted by the United States by reason of its adherence to the Articles of Agreement.

No part of the Articles gave a privileged position to the United States. The clause providing that a currency convertible into gold would be regarded as convertible within the meaning of the Articles was certainly designed to apply only to the United States. But the clause was fully justified as to its substance, and any member country could, theoretically, take advantage of it.

By contrast, the law authorizing the American president to ratify the Bretton Woods agreements did put the United States in a special position vis-à-vis other member countries. On the one hand, it stipulated that the American representatives on the Board of the Fund — and also on that of the World Bank — were to act under the authority of an interdepartmental coordinating committee. On the other hand, the approval of Congress would be required for any change in the parity of the dollar, that is, its parity in relation to gold.

The first of these requirements was only bothersome as a matter of principle. Theoretically the members of the Fund Board were supposed to act according to their judgment, not according to instructions from the government, or governments, which chose them. But in practice, as was only natural, they nearly all became spokesmen of the governments, so that the situation of the American representatives was not much different from that of their colleagues.

The second provision, on the contrary, was of great import.

The International Monetary Tangle

It is hard to see how the Fund could have functioned in practice if all countries had made changes in the parities of their currencies conditional on votes in their parliaments. The right which the American Congress reserved for itself made it moreover extremely difficult to activate the clause in the Articles concerning changes in the gold parities of all currencies. It was bound to be asked whether, indeed, the Americans accepted the idea that the laws of the new monetary order applied to them as well as to other countries.

Of all the equivocal features mentioned above, this last was probably the most troublesome. It was natural to leave open the matter of long- and medium-term international financial transactions which would someday be needed, as well as the techniques for executing them. It was natural not to pronounce, for the time being, on the means of achieving a reasonable degree of equilibrium in the capital components of balances of payments. It was quite natural not to try to define, except in the light of experience, what should be the obligations of "extreme creditors." It was at least acceptable to leave a certain ambiguity concerning the role remaining for monetary cooperation among a limited group of countries, especially European or Western monetary cooperation. It was a very serious matter, on the other hand, that the partners of the United States, at the very moment they engaged in the enterprise of the International Monetary Fund, had to wonder whether the Americans really accepted that the rules of the game should apply to themselves.

CHAPTER II

The Period before 1958

The First Years of the Bretton Woods Institutions

The Fund came into being progressively. It was only after the election of its third managing director, Per Jacobsson, in 1956 that its activities and its authority began to live up to what its founders had hoped for. While in the first years of its life the Fund, on the whole, conformed to the spirit of Bretton Woods, the period was marked by some developments not altogether in that spirit.

Shortly after it began operations, in June 1947 the Fund made a decision on gold policy, on the initiative of Great Britain supported by the USA, that was important in the sense that it showed for the first time that the Americans and the British were able, when they felt strongly about an issue, to force through an interpretation of the Articles contrary both to the letter and to the spirit of the Bretton Woods agreements. The Articles of the Fund provided that member countries could not buy gold above the parity price and could not sell it for less. On the other hand, they could sell it at a price above parity or buy it for less. That was only logical. The purchases and sales by public institutions ought to help to maintain the official price on the market; they should not contribute to moving the market price away from the official price. But Britain, which had not yet reopened the London gold market and which had been trying to prevent gold transactions in the sterling area, took a poor view of operations that took place, in spite of all its regulations, in some Asian and Near Eastern countries — operations that implicitly devalued the pound. The British thought they could get rid of these markets by depriving them of supplies. With American support they succeeded in getting the Fund Board to adopt a resolution forbidding member countries (consequently, producer countries, such as South Africa) from selling gold at a price above parity. This was an unfortunate decision, which resulted in a rise in the gold price on the free markets, and which was evaded by all sorts of tricky devices. It had to be revoked in September 1951.

The Fund's aptitude for exercising its powers in a case of devaluation was put to the test in 1949. The change in the parity of the pound sterling, involving changes in many other parities, was the first devaluation since World War II that was important for the whole international community. The experience was not very good. The new rate of exchange was, in fact, set by the British and the Americans. While the ministers of finance and governors of central banks of all the member countries were in session in Washington at the annual meeting of the Fund, the British Chancellor of the Exchequer, having agreed with his American colleague on a new parity, left for London on the Thursday, without even informing his other colleagues, who learned of the devaluation and new rate of exchange on the week-end. The new rate brought about a devaluation of the pound significantly greater than had generally been expected and considered reasonable. It placed the monetary authorities of most other countries in a dilemma. Should they remain attached to the pound and thus risk devaluing too much with respect to the dollar? Or should they break with the pound and thus risk having difficulty in exporting to the sterling area? The wise solution was to follow the pound down only part way. But the choice of an exact degree of devaluation was a very delicate one. The ministers and governors flew off to their respective capitals over the weekend to settle this vital and urgent problem. The new rate of exchange proposed by the British, and approved by the Americans, was naturally accepted by the Board of the Fund. In the following days most European countries made hasty decisions. As a result, some European currencies were probably devalued too much with respect to the dollar. The arrangements for the policing of exchange rates established at Bretton Woods had not worked satisfactorily.

The succeeding years were not marked by any major events for the Fund until 1958, when several important countries emerged from the so-called "transition" period and reestablished the convertibility of their currencies as provided by the Bretton Woods agreements. In the intervening years the Fund perfected its organization and little by little enhanced its authority.

Meanwhile, as is well known, the World Bank, mainly under the impetus provided by its third president, Mr. Eugene R. Black, became a remarkably active and effective instrument in the field of assistance to developing countries.

The Reawakening of European Monetary Cooperation

European monetary cooperation was reborn from the ashes of World War II, and reborn in a manner that involved a certain amount of American participation.

Between the two wars great steps had already been taken not only on the road to European cooperation but also toward a larger area of cooperation, involving the United States and even Japan. We mentioned earlier the establishment of the Bank for International Settlements, often known as the club of central banks. The United States and Japan were among its founders. There was also the Financial Committee of the League of Nations, which became a center for financial collaboration among governments, its work being particularly directed, it is true, toward the relaunching of the currencies of Eastern and Central Europe. Two large conferences — at Genoa in 1922 and at

The International Monetary Tangle

London in 1933 — had tried, albeit with little success, to respond to the prevailing sense that it had become necessary to establish some international monetary order among the principal countries. Finally, the Tripartite Agreement entered into by the governments of the United States, France, and Great Britain in 1936, and subsequently extended to several other European governments, might have marked the beginning of a durable coordination among the great financial centers. World War II put an end to that hope.

The Bretton Woods system, as outlined in 1944, was almost worldwide. Superimposed on it was an Anglo-American special relationship. The system left little room for any cooperation involving, alongside that between the British and the Americans, the countries of continental Europe (and eventually Japan). Why did things turn out differently from what was expected?

A primary reason was the spectacular setback to the Anglo-American grand design contained in the agreement of December 1945 — after Bretton Woods. Under that agreement, with the aid of the American loan to Britain, the pound was supposed to become convertible, that is, foreign holdings of sterling should again become freely exchangeable for any other currency, including the dollar. The credits were drawn on; the pound was made officially convertible. But the experiment soon led to intolerable losses of Britain's holdings of foreign exchange. In August 1947 the convertibility of the pound was suspended, not to be reestablished until 1958. At once the United States lost its taste for special assistance to Britain. Britain was forced to form a bloc with the other European countries in order to benefit from the Marshall Plan and thus cover her dollar requirements. She was likewise forced to set up camp under the same flag as the other European countries in order to finance her deficits in Europe.

Condemned to death at Bretton Woods, the BIS discovered that it had a hardy life. Its liquidation posed legal difficulties due to the fact, among others, that Germany, one of its founders and also in debt to it, no longer had a representative able to contract in that country's name. Unable to die, the BIS sought

to make itself useful. Thanks to the vision and ability of its
management, Maurice Frère, now president, and Roger Auboin,
managing director, the Bank was able to dissipate the unjusti-
fied charges leveled at it, to reestablish its credit in the United
States, and to make the large European central banks recognize
that for them Basel remained an invaluable center for joint action and mutual assistance. Even though American participation
in the BIS at the time consisted mostly of sympathetic gestures,
while Japan, by the Treaty of San Francisco, had given up its
status as a founding member, the Bank was back on the rails
and being made ready to play a role that would become more
important year by year.

When the Western European countries had been provided by
the Marshall Plan with dollars to pay for their purchases in the
United States and the rest of the outside world, they perceived
that intra-European trade was also giving rise to sizable deficits. With the reserves of most central banks reduced to in-
significance, and the dollars furnished by the Americans committed to payments to the dollar zone, there was no means of
covering these disequilibria. Paradoxically, it became easier
to finance deficits with the outside world than those within Europe. The OEEC[2] took hold of this problem, and with American support an ingenious solution was found.

As one consequence of the Marshall Plan, each beneficiary
country began to accumulate assets known as "counterpart
funds," consisting of the countervalue in national currency of
the dollar grants or loans of the American government. Under
the agreements entered into with the United States, that government had the right either to regard these balances as its own
property (as if it had bought the European currencies with dollars) or to control their use. It was decided to use part of these
funds to finance intra-European deficits, the Americans having
had the wisdom to understand that supporting the development
of trade among OEEC member countries was part and parcel

---

2. The Organization for European Economic Cooperation, created along
with the launching of the Marshall Plan, brought together the countries that
benefited from American aid, and also Switzerland.

of the drive for European recovery. So countries running a deficit with their European partners got, along with a dollar allocation as their direct share in Marshall aid, an allocation of European currencies, called a "European drawing right," to enable them to cover such a deficit. A committee of OEEC members was formed to deal with intra-European payments and their financing. This was one of the origins of what was to become the European Payments Union.

Another origin of the EPU is found in an initiative taken in 1947 by several continental members of the OEEC in an attempt to get away from the bilateralism still restricting trade and payments within Europe. It seemed paradoxical that a country with a surplus in its transactions with one partner should be unable to use it to settle a deficit with another. This continental group (Britain stayed out at first) elaborated a mechanism for multilateral compensation as a first effort to get away from bilateralism and out of the straitjacket it imposed on trade. To make this mechanism work there had to be an international agent responsible for following all the bilateral accounts and determining what compensations might be possible. The group of countries asked the BIS to assume this role, thus preparing it to become the agent for executing European monetary agreements.

The Marshall Plan being a one-time thing, it was clearly impossible to get in the habit of relying on the counterpart of American aid to finance intra-European disequilibria. In the normal course of events, the countries of the OEEC should be able to grant each other credits, provided their amounts remained within reasonable limits and provided that they were accompanied by sufficient discipline to make deficit countries improve their situation. Thus the European Payments Union was born through a natural evolution, and the BIS automatically became its agent. The EPU covered all the OEEC countries, including Switzerland. It provided for the opening of a credit by the EPU for each member, under which the EPU was obligated to lend to the member up to an agreed ceiling. It also provided for the possibility of credit "rallonges"[*] to be decided case by case. A certain proportion of each country's global surplus or deficit had to be settled in gold or in a currency equivalent to gold. Finally, the Management Committee of the EPU constituted for the member governments a permanent center for consultation on intra-European monetary relations in the broadest sense of that term.

The American government was not a member of the EPU. But the United States had favored and encouraged its creation, just as it had the first tentative moves toward multilateralization of intra-European payments. The EPU received an initial revolving fund in dollars drawn from Marshall Plan resources. And the United States had an observer on the Management Committee.

Life and Death of the European Payments Union

The EPU was a success.

During the decade of the 1950s it made possible first the multilateralization and ultimately the progressive elimination of import quotas that restricted trade expansion among OEEC members. The EPU's power to allocate resources to individual countries gave the OEEC a tool with which to enforce its objective of liberating intra-European trade and payments.

When first Germany, then France, then Britain experienced balance of payments crises, the EPU both helped to finance the deficits and, through its Management Committee, became the forum in which the country concerned could discuss with its partners its situation and measures of correction. The recommendations of the Management Committee had a salutary effect

---

*The French term "rallonge" was universally used in English texts or articles relating to the EPU for want of a satisfactory single English word to describe this operation. "Rallonge" combines the meanings of the phrases "stretch out" and "add to," as when one puts another piece into a dining room table to accommodate more guests — Translator.

on the governments and in each case strengthened the position of advocates of appropriate corrective measures.

Relations with the American government were good. At first the American Treasury, traditionally suspicious of any mechanism not founded on principles of nondiscrimination in trade and payments, looked on initiatives for European cooperation with a certain reserve; and the EPU did indeed rest on the notion that there should, for the time being at least, be greater freedom in intra-European relations than in those between Europe and the dollar zone. But the viewpoints of the State Department and of the Marshall Plan administrator were different, as were the personal views of Mr. John Snyder, secretary of the Treasury, and his closest advisors. Thanks to this kind of support, the EPU was born and prospered.

Relations with the IMF were also good. No doubt some elements of the Fund staff were reticent concerning the EPU and viewed without favor the birth of a system of monetary cooperation within Europe using as agent the BIS. But as the thing had been done, the Fund undertook the necessary collaboration with a good grace. One of its representatives attended meetings of the Management Committee as an observer. When France got into difficulty in 1957 and again in 1958, she was assisted jointly by the Fund and by the EPU, and the action of the two organizations was well coordinated.

Finally, and above all, within the Management Committee, in which all the Western European countries of financial importance participated, as well as in part the United States, there grew up habits of working together and reciprocal frankness that formed a precious asset for the future. The Committee, together with the monthly meetings of central bank governors in Basel, constituted two centers around which, as soon as all discrimination could be done away with, it became possible to envisage a new system of cooperation grouping the responsible authorities of all the great financial centers, including those of the United States and Canada.

Nevertheless, the EPU died one fine day without being replaced by anything of any significance.

As soon as Western Europe had recovered and most of the central banks had rebuilt their reserves, the Americans had every right to refuse any longer to accept discriminatory restrictions against the dollar affecting imports and financial transactions. The International Monetary Fund, for its part, had the right to expect that those European countries in the best position to do so should apply the clause of the Bretton Woods agreement providing for the convertibility of balances in national currencies held by foreigners. And Britain, which had reopened its gold market in 1954, was anxious to resume the abortive experiment of 1947, thus, by making foreign held sterling balances convertible into dollars, giving London a good chance to play once again a major international role.

The EPU was based on the idea, consistent with the facts of the immediate postwar period, of an OEEC monetary area within which imports and financial settlements (at least those for current accounts) would be progressively freed from all administrative restrictions. The moment the same freedom was extended to relations with the dollar zone, the concept of an OEEC monetary area disappeared. The very existence of the EPU was threatened.

Looking back at these events from today's vantage point, it seems that it would have been wise not to do away with the EPU without establishing some instruments of cooperation among the countries especially concerned about international capital movements. Knowing the amplitude of these movements during the past fifteen years and the severity of the problems posed by balances of payments on capital account, it is to be regretted that this was not done and that the Americans, and eventually the Canadians and the Japanese, were not invited to join such a cooperative venture, no longer as observers but as full partners.

Things did not turn out that way. To succeed the defunct EPU, the members of the OEEC limited themselves to concluding a European Monetary Agreement which envisaged nothing more than consultations among them. Except for a very vague clause, no provision was made for credits by, or for, members. The only resources available to the new mechanism were the initial funds inherited from the EPU. In fact, the sole function of the European Monetary Agreement turned out to be the granting of small credits to those OEEC members regarded as developing countries.

Why was the EPU liquidated in this way? The act can be explained as the sum of various factors.

The British did not like the idea of organs of international monetary cooperation other than the IMF. They had not given up their preference for a special Anglo-American relationship superimposed on the Fund. Their aim, furthermore, was to have the Fund evolve in a direction that would bring it closer to the formulae of the Keynes plan. They also expected to find in the Fund the means of alleviating the burden of the famous "sterling balances." In short, they saw the solution of their problems on the side of the Fund and of the United States.

The Americans had rallied to the concept of monetary cooperation within the orbit of the OEEC under the influence of the team responsible for administering the Marshall Plan and as a means of putting Europe back on its feet. That team had now been dispersed and their objective attained. In American eyes there was no reason to tack on to the Fund something else — something that might eventually involve obligations for the United States.

As for the management of the Fund, it could not help looking unfavorably on something that seemed to it to be competitive.

The continental Europeans, for their part, would have had the advantage of a mechanism providing an authority, and resources, that they would probably not get from the Fund. For their voices carried little weight in the Bretton Woods organizations. And if, in a reversal of trends that was always possible, they experienced large exports of capital to the United States, the utilization of their Fund quotas — assuming that it would have been possible[3] — would probably not have given them adequate foreign exchange reserves. Could they have made the liquidation of the EPU conditional on the establishment of other instruments more realistic than the European Monetary Agreement? There was no majority for making the attempt.

The EPU thus died in 1958. But not much time passed before it became apparent, and not only on the European shores of the Atlantic, that something was lacking in the international monetary system.

_____

3. It will be recalled that, in principle, the Fund's resources were reserved for the financing of deficits on current account. (See p. 10.)

CHAPTER III

From 1958 to 1971

During the whole of the period 1958-71, the United States ran a deficit in its balance of payments. Doubt about the equivalence between the dollar and gold, which first raised its head about 1960, spread right up to the moment in August 1971 when the nonconvertibility of the dollar was officially proclaimed. During all those years, if one abstracts from temporary deficits here or there due to exceptional circumstances, the balance of payments of each of the member states of the European Economic Community was in surplus and their reserves increased. Britain had a different experience, marked by a succession of exchange crises.

During this period the Monetary Fund engaged in two kinds of activities. One stemmed directly from the Bretton Woods agreements; the other arose from the new responsibilities it was given in 1968 at the time of the creation of the Special Drawing Rights. Leaving these new responsibilities on one side for the moment, it can be said that the Fund succeeded better and better in living up to the aspirations of its founders. Under the guiding force of two exceptionally capable managing directors, Per Jacobsson and Pierre Paul Schweitzer, both its authority and the volume of its operations grew. On three occasions the members agreed to a substantial increase in quotas.

And when in August 1971 the American government took the step already referred to, the Managing Director, to his great credit, made himself the spokesman for the community of members, expressing their concerns, particularly those of the developing countries. On the whole, events confirmed the quality of the work of the men who conceived the Fund.

The management of the World Bank and its affiliates during those thirteen years — as indeed during the previous fifteen — likewise did honor to the clear vision of the men of Bretton Woods. The Bank did, no doubt, face some serious difficulties because of the rates of interest it was obliged to ask from its borrowers and the need to keep within reasonable limits the burden of debt of the countries concerned. The Bank did the best it could under the circumstances, with the support of the governments of the lending countries.

The most interesting developments during the years immediately after 1958 were the tentative moves toward organizing new forms of collaboration between North America and Western Europe.

Efforts to Establish Monetary Cooperation
between North America and Western Europe (1958-65)

Because they were troubled by the U. S. balance of payments, the Americans came around to the idea of a special form of cooperation with the financial centers of Western Europe, Canada, and Japan. It is instructive to recall the successive steps they were led to take in that direction under the lash of necessity, and also to look at the limits they took care not to overstep.

The first sign was the revival of their interest in the Bank for International Settlements. We have noted that after the war the United States had scarcely gone beyond some gestures of courtesy and sympathy. The Federal Reserve System, for example, had not thought that it should occupy the two seats on the Board of the BIS to which it was entitled. When the dollar

balances of the main creditor central banks, and the gold
purchases of some of them, began to grow, the United
States saw that there would be advantages for it in some
arrangements by which these banks could avoid risk on the
exchange value of the dollar. The Americans discovered
the virtues of the technique of "swaps," which the European
central banks had used among themselves for a long time. The
monthly meetings in Basel, attended by the governors of most
of the central banks with which the United States hoped to work
out swap arrangements, were an ideal place to negotiate appropriate agreements. A whole network of swaps was woven between the Federal Reserve Bank of New York and its European
correspondents. The representatives of the New York Fed
were to be seen crossing the Atlantic almost every month to
participate in the Basel weekends. Representatives of the Board
of Governors of the Federal Reserve System in Washington
showed more and more interest. Before long the Americans became de facto members of the Club of Basel, which was shortly
enriched by the adhesion of the Canadians and the reentry of
the Japanese. Thus cooperation among the main central banks
of the industrial countries seemed to be getting under way. Despite all this the Americans refrained from occupying the seats
to which they were entitled on the board of the BIS. This was
perhaps because they thought that such a move would be contrary to the principle that they should not recognize officially
any machinery for international monetary cooperation except
the IMF, a principle which they believed to be embodied in the
plans passed by the Congress.

The second sign was the transformation of the OEEC in 1961
into a larger body called the Organization for Economic Cooperation and Development (OECD), with the United States as a
member. This was a logical move because the OEEC became
largely superfluous once its members were almost all either
in the European Economic Community or the European Free
Trade Association. One of the reasons motivating the Americans was the hope that in the new organization there could be

a better coordination of bilateral assistance to developing countries and more of a European contribution. But they also thought that the new organization might become a place where national policies, especially policies designed to influence broad economic fluctuations and financial policies, could be discussed and compared, thus encouraging their European partners to adopt an understanding and cooperative attitude toward America's problems.

If the Americans had followed this reasoning to its natural conclusion, they would have joined the European Monetary Agreement, which provided, at least on paper, for coordination in monetary matters among the members and which would thus have become an OECD monetary agreement. From the very beginning of the discussions on the charter of the new organization, they insisted that it should contain no monetary clauses insofar as it applied to them. Thus it was accepted that the European Monetary Agreement would stay as it was under the OEEC and apply only to the European members of the new organization. The Americans came in, but they did not come all the way in.

Very soon the OECD set up a small committee, known as Group No. 3 of the Economic Policy Committee, in which representatives of all the financial centers met. Here the custom of exchanging views on governments' economic policies became established. Monetary policies were often brought up. However, most of the time the discussions were rather platonic. Unlike the Management Committee of the defunct EPU, the participants in Group No. 3 had no power to back their recommendations by decisions to grant or refuse financial support.

The United States was induced to make another move by a difficulty which, in truth, preoccupied the British as much, if not more, than themselves. Because of the growing dollar glut throughout the world, clients of the IMF tended to prefer to purchase from the Fund the currencies of the countries of the European Economic Community. As those countries' quotas were not very big, the Fund's holdings of their currencies were

29

constantly on the verge of running out. This did not suit the plans of the British who were preparing, around 1960, to draw heavily on the Fund. The Americans, for their part, while in principle excluding any possibility of drawing for their own account, became uneasy about a situation which might become irksome to them.[4]

Early in 1961 the idea was floated of activating a clause in the Articles of Agreement allowing the Fund to borrow supplementary resources from some of its members. The Fund would borrow resources from the countries of the Common Market and use them to meet the drawings of other countries, in particular, the expected British drawing. A corresponding undertaking to lend supplementary resources to the Fund would be made by Britain and the United States, which for the time being would be a dead letter.

The members of the Common Market had no reason to favor a formula that would result in their putting up supplementary resources without having control over their uses. The question was raised as to whether it might not be better to deal with the problem in the OECD framework, which encompassed precisely the countries likely to be involved in these supplementary credit arrangements. Under such a setup the lenders could establish certain conditions.

The Americans and the British ceded some ground in the face of the reservations expressed by the Common Market countries, particularly France, in the person of Wilfrid Baumgartner, then Minister of Finance. The matter was settled by a compromise toward the end of 1961, which largely satisfied the continental Europeans. The supplementary resources would still be borrowed by the Fund, but they would not be mingled with its other resources. The manner of their employment would be discussed with the lending countries. For this purpose a group of those

---

4. It was obviously because of these British and American concerns that about this time (July 1961) the Fund reversed the interpretation of its statutes made, on American initiative, in 1946, whereby its resources must, in principle, be reserved for use in covering deficits on current account. (See p. 10.)

Fund members willing, when the time should come, to provide
supplementary resources, within agreed limits, was organized
outside the formal structure of the Fund. This was the substance of what became known as the General Arrangements to
Borrow (GAB). Thus was born the Group of Ten, which included
Belgium, Britain, Canada, the Federal Republic of Germany,
France, Italy, Japan, the Netherlands, Sweden, and the United
States — later joined by Switzerland, even though it is not a
member of the Fund.

Thus the Americans and the British accepted the principle
of a system of special monetary cooperation among ten, or
rather eleven, governments. But they accepted it in a somewhat ambiguous form because the Group of Ten (as it continued
to be called) was only partly distinct from the Fund and constituted a small club inside the big club. This ambiguity ultimately
gave birth to many problems.

Developments in the gold market soon led the United States
to take one further step to strengthen cooperation among central banks on the two sides of the Atlantic.

As the main gold market was in London, it was traditionally
the Bank of England that kept an eye on the market, asking other
central banks, when necessary, to moderate or stretch out their
purchases. When the market surged in October 1960, pushing
the price well over the official $35 an ounce, the Americans
were sufficiently frightened to be persuaded by the British to
make some of their gold available for sale through the market.
After that the market settled down to an equilibrium, which allowed for normal purchases by central banks. A problem arose,
however, because the poor coordination of central bank purchases risked provoking, from time to time, temporary ex-
cesses of demand in relation to supply. But it was in the general interest to avoid even brief breaks above the parity price.

It appeared that the principal central banks would benefit if
they could get together to introduce some discipline into their
gold operations. It also appeared that the market was, fundamentally, in an equilibrium that permitted net annual purchases

by the central banks of the Basel Club. It seemed reasonable, therefore, for these banks to make advances to the market when needed in order to keep the price stable. Such interventions did not seem likely to involve any very large resources. This was the origin of an agreement reached in Basel in 1962 among most of the central banks in the Basel Club, including the Federal Reserve Bank of New York. It was agreed that, through the intermediary of the Bank of England, banks proposing to buy metal, instead of competing with each other, would divide among themselves, according to a rule of thumb, whatever amount the state of the market permitted to be bought without destabilizing the price. It was further agreed that metal could be temporarily released to the market when needed, up to an agreed maximum, and that the resources required would be put up by the members of the club according to an agreed formula (the United States' proportion being 50 percent).

This arrangement, known as the "gold pool," is doubly interesting: first, because the Americans were in it along with the Europeans, and second, because it worked very well. It worked well, that is, until those days in 1967 when the market's equilibrium was shattered by so severe a decline of confidence in the dollar that any notion that sales by the central banks could be regarded as "temporary" became nonsensical.

It was also in 1962 that discussions began about an eventual reform of the international monetary system. During their first phase, at least, these discussions seemed to reinforce the cooperation among the Eleven.

As early as 1961 Jacques Rueff, in an article which had wide repercussions, had declared war on the damage being perpetrated by the growing accumulations of dollars by central banks and had recommended a return to the gold standard, recognizing that this implied a substantial increase in the official gold price. Beginning in 1963, the French government, somewhat more modestly, started to denounce what it considered to be the defects in the method of financing the American deficit by a continuous growth in short-term credits granted by central banks, especially by means of increases in their dollar balances. It undertook to stop this process, at least as far as France was concerned, both by buying gold from the United States and by prepaying some of its dollar debts. The French suggested that there should be concerted action designed, in a first stage, to put a stop to the increase in the short-term indebtedness of the United States and, in a second stage, to soak up any excessive foreign holdings of dollars.

Moved by a very different set of preoccupations, several economists, mainly in Britain, launched a campaign in 1962 to bring about a change in the rules of the International Monetary Fund designed to remove the alleged danger of a shortage of international liquidity. They took up some of Keynes's ideas on the inadequacy of gold as a constituent of reserves, on the risk of worldwide deflation, and on the need for a deliberate creation of fiduciary reserves by the Fund. The British government limited itself to proposing a formula under which the Fund would assist deficit countries to finance themselves by increased debts expressed in their own currencies associated with exchange rate guarantees — a suggestion presented by the Chancellor of the Exchequer at the annual meeting of the governors of the Fund in September 1962.

The American government, at first unfavorable to changes in the existing regime, about which it had no reason to complain, finally agreed to the idea of carrying out an intensive study of the system and its possible defects. On its initiative it was decided to assign that study to the Group of Ten. This body got to work in 1963. It had a difficult task. While most of its members agreed on the principle of a revision of the system, the Anglo-Americans and the continental Europeans wanted changes for reasons that were directly opposed.

The only recommendation on which the Group of Ten reached fairly rapid agreement was the adoption in 1964 of the suggestion that there should be instituted what was called "multilateral surveillance" of developments affecting international

liquidity.[5] The idea was that the governments and central banks
of the Eleven would follow developments affecting international
liquidity, especially the short-term indebtedness of the United
States, and take whatever measures might become necessary
to prevent anarchy. This decision, on paper at least, was a
tribute to the virtues of collaboration among the Eleven. Unhappily, this multilateral surveillance remained in the realm
of ideas. For it to make sense, the members of the club would
have had to stop enabling the United States to add to its short-
term indebtedness. France did so. But most of her partners
failed to follow suit. That was particularly the case of the principal creditors of the United States, to wit, the Federal Republic of Germany, Italy, and Japan. Long after these events it became known that the Bundesbank had been led to make a secret
promise to the Americans not to ask for conversion of its dollars into gold. Multilateral surveillance therefore remained a
dead letter through the joint faults of those who did not want it
to work and those who thought it was impossible to make it
work. And the Americans continued to finance the greater part
of their annual deficits by increasing international liquidity.

To adopt as an objective the achievement of a more adequate
level of international liquidity logically requires one to tackle
two problems: to prevent excessive liquidity and to see that it
grows fast enough. In 1963-64 the first problem made its presence painfully felt; the second, for the time being, was academic. Nevertheless it was on the second problem that the
Group of Ten concentrated practically all of its time and effort.
The notion that liquidity could simply be created by concerted
action whetted the appetites of both the reserve currency countries and the developing countries. Furthermore, it was impossible to refuse to discuss liquidity creation without being
accused of paving the way for a world crisis of deflation and

5. It was about then that we adopted the habit of using this expression, in-
vented by the economists, to describe the totality made up of central bank
reserves plus the other resources of foreign exchange available to the various countries, in particular, the foreign exchange holdings of their banking
systems.

unemployment. Thus, having disposed of the first problem by setting up the "multilateral surveillance," the Group of Ten spent four years working on the second. They were four utterly confusing years, during which some participants at times did not know what their doctrine was, several changed their views along the way, and France distinguished herself by a switch of position that helped her to earn, at the end of the day, a resounding defeat.

Ignoring the details of the struggle, we may say that it revolved around the opposition between two extreme positions, which were approximately as follows.

According to one view there could be no question of creating new kinds of reserves as long as the United States, as a matter of policy, continued to generate a superabundance of liquidity. Studying, as a precaution, what might happen if the American balance of payments turned around was, of course, admissible. Given the hypothesis, adopted at the start, of no change in the gold price and supposing that European countries decided that they would no longer hold more dollars than they needed for working balances, there could come a time when some fiduciary element would have to be added to gold in suitable amounts in order to permit all members of the international community to hold adequate reserves. This fiduciary element should be as like gold as possible. The salutary discipline which the risk of gold losses imposes on deficit nations should be preserved. Deficit countries should therefore be required to use, pari passu, their gold and their fiduciary reserves. Finally, the fiduciary element must enjoy good credit. It must therefore constitute a claim against only those central banks that were members of the Group of Ten, which, in turn, would be the only ones to hold it as reserves, thus freeing some gold for use by the rest of the international community. In short, what would be involved would be reciprocal multilateral credits among the Eleven.

According to the opposing view, a mechanism for creating multilateral fiduciary reserves to add to gold and dollars (which both would continue to be used as reserves) should be established and put to work at once so that it might be tested and put in order. It would be improper for the new system to not benefit all members of the Fund in the same way. The creation of new fiduciary reserves should therefore take place in the framework of the Fund, and each member country should be expected to participate as both debtor and creditor. In view of the fact that many developing countries held almost no gold in their reserves, a pari passu relationship between payments out of fiduciary reserves and payments in gold would be out of the question. Furthermore, that would be too complex to arrange among so many countries. But the Fund would be given the responsibility for keeping track of the composition of each country's reserves and using its authority to see to it that countries whose reserves increased accepted suitable amounts of the new international money.

At the start of negotiations the French position was close to the first of these theses. The other members of the European Community, aware that the new money would quickly flow toward them, adopted positions not differing much from that of the French, though somewhat softer. The Americans, who at first were not very favorable to the creation of a reserve unit that might dethrone the dollar, appeared hesitant in the face of this common front.

It was not out of the question that a compromise on this matter might be reached, somewhat analogous to that of 1961, whereby it was agreed to furnish the Fund with supplementary resources of currencies of which it was short. As we have seen, that compromise gave a blessing to monetary cooperation within the framework of the Eleven while respecting the sensitivities of the rest of the international community, and those of the Fund.

If things had turned out that way, cooperation among the Eleven might have become a serious affair. One could even have spoken of general economic cooperation among the Eleven. For about this same time the trade negotiations known as the Kennedy Round were reaching their end. The agreement that emerged from those negotiations reflected mainly the discussions involving the European Economic Community, Britain, the United States, Japan, Canada, Sweden, and Switzerland. It was, in fact, very largely a trade agreement among the Eleven.

From 1958 to 1971

The Decline of Cooperation
among the Eleven (1965-71)

In 1965 things began to happen that were gradually to reduce monetary collaboration among the Eleven almost to a façade. These developments were the combined product of increasing misunderstandings among the Common Market countries and a determination by the United States, which became more and more evident, not to be obliged to alter its policy in response to external constraints.

As early as the beginning of 1965, France, in the person of President de Gaulle, took a position leaning toward a reestablishment of the gold standard. Though it was not put in so many words, the notion of a revaluation of the metal was implied. In June of that same year France quit the Brussels organizations for several months because of quarrels with her Common Market partners over "supranationality" and thus ceased to participate in the Community discussions designed to define a position for the Six in the international monetary negotiations. At the beginning of 1966 France got a new finance minister who soon let it be known that, in his opinion, central banks should have no reserves other than gold, supplemented, when there were deficits to be covered, by conventional credits from the International Monetary Fund. France accepted the idea that for this purpose the Fund's resources should be increased. In early 1967 the French government notified its Common Market partners of this new position through diplomatic channels, which meant that it no longer accepted the idea, even for some future time, of the collective creation of a fiduciary component of reserves, even if such component were to be used only pari passu with gold, and even if its creation were to be restricted to the Eleven. That position also indicated, although this was not said officially, that Paris hoped for a change in the official gold price.

It was also in 1965 that the Americans began to tilt their position, but in a wholly different direction. Up to then, as we have noted, they had shown little interest in the creation of a

37

new component for reserves because they felt they could count on continuing to finance their deficits bilaterally. But in 1965, alarmed by the outlook for their balance of payments and by the size of the dollar debt payable on demand or at short term they were in danger of accumulating, alarmed also by the threat to their freedom of action posed by a revival of support for the gold standard, the Americans announced that henceforth they would favor the creation of a reserve instrument of a collective character. From that time on all their efforts were devoted to seeing to it that such a reserve instrument should be created, that it should be done quickly, that it should be done on a world-wide scale within the Fund framework, and that its use should not be tied to a parallel use of gold reserves. In getting this thesis accepted they had the developing countries for allies.

The Common Market countries other than France found themselves in an extremely uncomfortable negotiating posture, as they agreed neither with the new French position nor with the Americans. They maneuvered as best they could, but it was very difficult for them to hold out. After a series of flareups, the agreement calling for the creation of the celebrated Special Drawing Rights was reached at Stockholm in April 1968. The American thesis prevailed. But there were a few concessions to the continental Europeans. The only one of real significance was that according to which the creation of SDRs had to be approved by an 85 percent vote of the Fund Board, which gave the Six a right of veto, assuming they could achieve unanimity among themselves. France could not accept such an agreement without disavowing her position. So even though all her Common Market associates accepted, France refused to adhere.

The concept of a special degree of cooperation among the Eleven thus received a very hard blow. The solidarity of the Six was shattered and was not reestablished until 1969, when, because of the deterioration of her financial situation in the wake of the "events of May" 1968, France was no longer able to stay apart from the Stockholm agreement.

From 1958 to 1971

It was also in the spring of 1968 that the cooperation among the Eleven in the gold market ended. The massive speculative demand for gold sparked by the growing doubts about the dollar during 1967 left no place for net purchases by the central banks of the Group of Ten. The notion of temporary sales on the market thus lost all meaning. Nevertheless the Americans pressed the central banks hard to continue, for at least a while, in order to hold the price at par, to sell gold that they would have no chance to recover. This went farther than had been envisaged when the gold pool was created, and the Bank of France refused to go along with these tactics. When it became evident toward the end of 1967 and the beginning of 1968 that such sales were absurd, the obvious solution was to abandon them while preserving the other aspect of the 1962 agreement, namely, that the central banks of the Basel Club should work together on questions affecting the gold market. But the United States wanted something more. Two meetings of the central banks concerned were held away from Basel, without the Bank of France, which was not invited. During the first meeting the United States got the group to agree to continue the policy of sales, which soon led to insupportable losses of gold. At the second meeting, held in March 1968 in Washington, a very confused communiqué was adopted, proclaiming that henceforth the free market would be separated from the official market and left to itself and, in addition, that the stocks of gold held by the central banks were considered to be adequate. This declaration was presented to the world as meaning that the banks which met in Washington intended that no new metal would be added to their reserves of monetary gold and that, in consequence, they supported a progressive reduction in the monetary role of gold.

This was a new blow to cooperation among the Eleven. The Americans had convened the club in Washington, excluding one of its members, to get out of them an equivocal declaration that they then interpreted as fully supporting their views. This was not in the spirit of the Club of Basel, into which the Americans had been welcomed wholeheartedly and treated as full members.

The International Monetary Tangle

We must finally mention the dilatory attitude of the Eleven with respect to one very important question. They not only failed to solve the problem of the Eurodollar. They did not even come up with possible solutions. But if there was any matter within their competence, this was it.

These things will be difficult to explain to future historians: why the banks in countries of the Group of Ten, other than the United States, freely opened their books to dollar deposits and to loans in dollars; why they were able to offer interest rates higher than those in the United States; why they were able to make dollar credits of all sorts that evaded the surveillance of any central banks and competed in each country with credits that were subject to strict central bank regulations; why some central banks, including some of the Eleven, thought it convenient to place some of their own dollar holdings in this Eurodollar market, thus feeding those banking channels that were outside the control of national monetary authorities and frustrating national monetary policies; why, through the Eurodollar channel, it became possible to create money and transform short-term into long-term credits with no brake other than the sense of moderation of private banks; why the Eurodollar phenomenon, after beginning modestly around 1960, grew progressively to enormous figures (nearly $60 billion for all "Eurocurrencies" by 1970, of which about $50 billion were U.S. dollars); and why the machinery for cooperation among the Eleven never went to the heart of the problem.

There are some excuses that can be made for this indigence. For one thing, as most national money markets were curtailed by regulations or hindrances, the Eurodollar provided an unmatchable instrument for international financing. This amounts to saying that the preponderance of the dollar as Europe's transnational currency is to be explained, to a certain extent, by the Europeans' ineptitude in providing themselves with monetary systems that responded to the requirements of international finance — which is not very complimentary to the Europeans. A second excuse is that measures of surveillance would have made sense only if applied to all markets in which the

40

phenomenon had developed, failing which the market would simply move to the least controlled markets, to the detriment of the banks of other countries. But some members of the Group of Ten were not prepared to apply control measures. This excuse is valid. But it amounts only to saying that on this great problem there was a lack of cooperative spirit.

Passive in the face of the growing American indebtedness, passive before the rising tide of Eurodollars, between 1968 and 1970 the Eleven awaited the storm, holding their customary meetings on schedule at the level of ministers or that of central bank governors. The most notable event was a session held in November 1968 intended, by those who initiated it, to agree on an upward valuation of the mark and a devaluation of the French franc. At the end of the meeting, at which the atmosphere was particularly unpleasant, both the franc and the mark came out with unchanged parities.

But the dollar could not go on getting weaker and weaker without the increasingly fictitious character of its alleged convertibility finally being publicly recognized.

In the spring of 1971, responding to domestic economic considerations, the American authorities relaxed their monetary policy. At the same time, determined to fight inflation, the German authorities hardened theirs. The increased spread between interest rates in the two markets provoked a new flood of dollars into the coffers of the Bundesbank, which in early May was forced to shut down the foreign exchange market and stop buying dollars at a fixed rate. Austria and Switzerland promptly revalued their currencies upward.

The final stage was reached in August 1971, when the convertibility of the American currency was suspended sine die.

One might then have imagined a devaluation of the dollar accompanied by a revision upward or downward of the parities of a certain number of other currencies; the Fund's agreement could easily have been obtained. One might also have imagined that the United States would seek the authorization of the Fund to let its currency remain inconvertible and floating for a while, until it would become easier to choose a new parity; the Fund's agreement to this could also doubtless have been obtained. It was obvious, however, that neither of these two formulas corresponded to the views of Congress, which had always rejected any notion that Federal policy could be subordinated to the Fund's authority. Thus as soon as circumstances arose that would have resulted in such subordination, the Bretton Woods agreements collapsed.

The American government said as much, in effect, and at the same time placed a ten percent surcharge on all imports. In its view a profound revision of international monetary relationships had become a self-evident necessity. The Americans advanced a few, actually rather confused, ideas which they seemed to hold as to the nature of such a revision. And they seemed determined to persuade their partners to accept them. A new era was beginning.

CHAPTER IV

Since 1971

A Glance at the Period as a Whole

"What has been done so far in the way of organizing the international economy has been unfairly burdensome for the United States and must be recast; the solution of the problem of the American deficit will require unilateral trade concessions to the United States by its partners; central banks must stop intervening in exchange markets; they must not prevent 'clean floating' from setting a proper value for one currency in terms of others, in particular a proper value for the dollar; they must not practice 'dirty floating' by intervening to prevent exchange rates from rising or falling in response to the free play of market forces; the whole policy followed in the past by the American authorities, in collaboration with the other central banks of the Basel Club, designed to reduce artificially the pressures on the dollar by means of loans, is unhealthy and must be abandoned; and since the Bretton Woods agreements have collapsed, they should be sent back to the drawing board; the international monetary system must be adapted to the realities of the day, particularly by incorporating constraints on creditor countries."

This, in substance, is the language heard by the world in

The International Monetary Tangle

August 1971, and during the following months, from the spokesmen for the United States, particularly from the mouth of Mr. John
Connally, then secretary of the Treasury.

Following such a profession of faith, one might have expected
during the period ahead strong fluctuations in the exchange
value of the dollar. One might also have expected a reform con-
ferring increased power on the International Monetary Fund,
possibly including the right to propose — if not to impose —
changes up or down in the parities of currencies. One might,
finally, have considered it likely that there would be a greater
solidarity among the European countries in the face of the
problems posed for them by Washington's new policy.

We can see today that whereas up to about 1973 these ex-
pectations seemed to be at least partially fulfilled, developments since then have followed a very different course. Since
the middle of 1975 the dollar's value in relation to the mark,
and in relation to the yen, has not changed very much. The ambitious
project of elaborating a new international monetary charter
proved abortive. The modifications in the Bretton Woods agreements that were agreed consisted mostly of taking note of the
new de facto relationships among currencies. Finally, from the
monetary viewpoint the European Economic Community today
finds itself more divided than ever. The Federal Republic of
Germany is a bastion of exchange stability and relatively modest price increases; Britain and Italy, racked by inflation, have
let their currencies float downward for several years; while
France seems to be in an intermediate position.

Why did things turn out this way?

One part of the explanation is obviously to be sought in the
oil crisis and the increases in the prices of petroleum products
that began in the autumn of 1973. Even though this crisis did
not spare the United States, a large petroleum importer, it had
the effect of improving the position of the dollar. By the end of
1973 it had become apparent that the balances of payments of
Britain, France, Italy, and Japan were hurt more by the hike in
oil prices than that of the United States. It also became clear
during 1974 that the huge accumulations of dollars by the oil-

44

exporting countries were being invested largely in the United States or on the Eurodollar market. Even though the banks that got these dollar deposits reloaned a large proportion of them abroad, the whole effect was to strengthen the position of the American currency in relation to those of Europe and the yen.

A second explanation may be sought in the general evolution of the world economy in recent years. In its first phase the policy of stimulation adopted by the U. S. authorities in 1971 in order to reverse a decline in the growth rate, which was followed throughout 1972, prevented the devaluation of the dollar from having a quick impact on the American balance of payments. But this policy was progressively reversed after the middle of 1973. Monetary management became very strict in 1974, when it became necessary to combat an unprecedented rate of inflation, and remained cautious when an economic recovery in mid-1975 made it important to discourage a new round of price increases. In the meantime the slow pace of the economy during 1974 and 1975 put a strong brake on U. S. imports. The balance of payments improved and the dollar strengthened.

Nevertheless, neither the oil crisis nor the business cycle would have produced these results if there had not been, in addition, a progressive change in the attitude of the American authorities away from that of the summer and autumn of 1971. Not only was a much larger emphasis given to the struggle against internal inflation as an objective of economic policy. Those authorities also began to realize the inconveniences that would arise from actual application of the doctrine of "clean floating." Bit by bit they came around to the belief that a regime of floating currencies necessarily calls for some controls, if erratic speculative movements of funds capable of generating dangerous and excessive effects are to be avoided. Were they aware of all the technical implications for their own policies of this development in their ideas? One may well ask, and we will come back to this point later. It remains true that one of the keys to understanding the complex developments that occurred on the world monetary scene after 1971 is to be found in the modification of certain American conceptions.

The principal events of the period were: the devaluation by steps, followed by the progressive stabilization, of the dollar; the growing divergency in the behavior of the currencies of Western Europe; the setback to projects for the construction of a new world monetary charter; the augmented role of the dollar as a pillar of the de facto monetary regime that had come about; and finally, the evolution that seemed to be taking place in the methods of international monetary cooperation.

The Vicissitudes of the Dollar

It seems possible to distinguish three phases in the curve formed by fluctuations in the effective exchange rate[6] of the dollar since 1971: a devaluation phase that reached its maximum in mid-1973; a phase of sizable up-and-down fluctuations that lasted through the autumn of 1975; and since then a phase of relative stability that there is some basis for hoping — although we cannot be sure — will last for a while.

The devaluation phase itself, which ran from mid-1971 to mid-1973, took place in three steps. The first was marked by the Smithsonian Agreement of December 1971, a product of the reaction of the United States' partners in the Group of Ten against the floating of the dollar as envisaged by Mr. Connally. The dollar was devalued by about 8 percent, while several currencies were revalued upward (in particular, the yen by 7.7 percent and the mark by 4.6 percent); and the 10 percent American surtax on imports was abolished. But the operation yielded only a respite. Throughout 1972, despite several declarations by the Eleven of their determination to defend the new rates and despite a resumption by the United States in July 1972

---

6. After a general adjustment of exchange rates, specialists calculate for each currency what percentage of unilateral adjustment of the rate for that currency would have produced an effect on the balance of payments of the country in question equivalent to that produced by the general shifting of rates. The result of this calculation yields the effective exchange rate.

46

Since 1971

of the swap arrangements it had condemned in 1971, it was
clear that the elements required for a real correction were
not yet in place. This was not surprising. The degree of effective devaluation of the dollar was probably insufficient; Washington had not made the slightest commitment to defend the new
rate; the easy money policy of the United States continued; and
the American trade deficit persisted. When a new crisis broke
at the beginning of February 1973, making it necessary on February 10 to close the exchange markets, the United States, with
the agreement of its partners, decided on a further devaluation
of 10 percent. Despite this amputation — which in this case
probably was adequate — confidence had been so shattered that
the defense of the new rate had to be quickly abandoned. By the
end of March the dollar had rejoined the tribe of floating currencies. Soon this floating dollar took a sharp plunge. On July
6, 1973, the effective exchange rate of the dollar had fallen another 9 percent from the March level. This was the third step
in the devaluation of the dollar. The level reached was absurd.
The drop had manifestly been excessive.

From July 1973 until the autumn of 1975, the American currency fluctuated widely in both directions. The beginning of the
period was notable for a meeting of the Group of Ten, during
which the American representatives showed evidence of a firm
intention not to leave the exchange market to its own devices
and proceeded to increase the size of the swap agreements they
had concluded with other central banks. A quick recovery followed, soon to be reinforced by some tightening of the Federal
Reserve Board's monetary policy and by the favorable effect
on the dollar of the oil crisis. By the end of January 1974 the
effective exchange rate for the dollar had risen by 17 percent,
almost reaching the level of December 1971. But the situation
soon turned around, under the impact in particular of the re-
moval of controls on American capital exports. In May 1974
the effective rate for the dollar had fallen again by 9 percent.
In September 1974 it rose again by 6 percent following a reflux
of funds provoked by some banking troubles in Europe. By February 1975, for a variety of technical reasons, it had lost nearly

47

9 percent by comparison with September 1974 and was nearly
back to the low level of July 1973. Then a number of favorable
factors cropped up, including the publication of figures con-
firming an improvement in the U. S. balance of trade. By September 1975 not only had the preceding drop been wiped out,
but the dollar had come to within 3 percent of the value vis-à-
vis other currencies that had been fixed in December 1971.

All these oscillations in the effective exchange rate (which
is a weighted average) naturally involved much greater variations in the rate of the dollar against some currencies, notably
the mark and the Swiss franc.

Were all these ups and downs, and the operational and psychological disturbances they caused, really necessary? We
will return to this question. In any case, by the middle of 1975
more and more authoritative voices were being heard, in both
the United States and Europe, expressing the view that the time
had come to tighten controls on the floating exchange rates in
some fashion that would avoid, so far as possible, erratic variations of mainly speculative origin. This trend of thought has
certainly not been unrelated to the fact that since September
1975 the fluctuations of the dollar against the currencies of the
European "snake" and against the yen have been kept within
narrower limits. The question posed is how long this phase of
greater stability of the dollar will last. The answer, as we
shall see, does not depend exclusively on the United States
but does depend on it to a large degree.

The Divergent Behavior of the European Currencies

In the course of the period 1971-76, the behavior of the currencies of Western Europe became more and more divergent.

Faced by the suspension of dollar convertibility and the hard-
ening of American policy, the members of the European Economic Community were able to restore a certain degree of
unity of views during the second half of 1971. After the December 1971 devaluation of the dollar, they agreed on a technical

arrangement, to which Britain adhered, designed to limit the margins within which their currencies would fluctuate against each other.[7] This harmony did not last long.

As early as June 1972 the British authorities decided to let sterling float, and the effective exchange rate for that currency has fallen steeply from that moment on, dropping more rapidly in the spring of 1973 and again in 1976. But, after all, Britain had long practiced a monetary policy differing from those of the principal continental countries. In a sense the direction taken by the lira at the beginning of 1973 was more disappointing. Because of political, social, and financial difficulties, the Italian authorities had to resign themselves to permitting their currency to float. The effective exchange value of the lira has hardly paused in its depreciation since then, following a general path not very different from that of sterling.

Deprived of the presence of the Italians, but benefiting from that of Denmark, joined later by Norway and Sweden, the founder members of the European Economic Community decided in March 1973 to maintain as among themselves the grouping of currencies known as the "snake." It was agreed that fluctuations of these currencies with respect to each other would be kept within fixed limits by means of concerted interventions in the market, while, with respect to the dollar, they would move as a group.

The link thus established between the mark and the French franc posed a problem from the very beginning because of the great disparity between the two countries, ever since the war, in their struggle against inflation. From the autumn of 1973 onward, the difficulty was aggravated by the fact that the French balance of payments was much more severely damaged by the repercussions of the oil crisis than that of Germany. In the event, up to the summer of 1976 the franc's destiny lay between that of the mark and that of the floating currencies. It left the

---

7. Because of the widening to 2.25 percent in the allowable margin for fluctuations against the dollar (part of the Washington agreement), the European currencies could have fluctuated as much as 4.5 percent up or down in relation to each other in default of some special arrangement.

"snake" in February 1974, returned in July 1975, and got out again in March 1976. But after July 1976 the French franc began to decline vis-à-vis both the "snake" and the dollar, rejoining the company of the lira and the pound, although not depreciating as much as those currencies. During the same period the Spanish peseta continued to decline, while the Swiss franc showed even more strength than the mark.

This division of Western European currencies into two groups, one of relatively stable currencies, the other of more or less soft ones, reflected a phenomenon that was not new: the unequal capacities of two groups of countries to preserve the internal purchasing power of their currencies. But even if the regime of floating exchange rates was not responsible for this situation, it served to aggravate it. The appreciation of their currencies helped the Federal Republic of Germany and those countries more or less linked to her economy to more nearly master inflation. By contrast, the fall in the value of the currencies of countries in the other group was promptly reflected in the prices of their imports, which stimulated the general rise in prices. The regime of floating underlined and enlarged the split in Western Europe.

The Reform of the International Monetary System

As we have seen, after August 1971 the United States took the position that the Bretton Woods agreements had collapsed — collapsed, at least, so far as any of their clauses might conflict with Washington's new policy. As a consequence the dispositions concerning convertibility, the stability of exchange rates, and the role of gold, the very essence, that is, of the Fund's Articles, were to be regarded as passé. When M. Pierre Paul Schweitzer, the managing director of the Fund, in conformity with the duties of his office, reminded the Americans of some of their international commitments, particularly their obligation to establish a new parity for the dollar, they let it be known that they would veto a renewal of his appointment, which was to end in 1973, and they did so.

Should a new charter be drawn up and substituted for the old one? Or, since the existing charter was already largely dormant, should the world live for the time being under a de facto regime? At the outset the first formula was favored. With the exception of a few points, the second prevailed.

In proposing to recast the Articles, the United States had two main objects in view. It wanted to give the Fund a means of exerting sufficient pressure on creditor countries to oblige them to modify their policies and eventually to revalue their currencies. For this the Fund would have to be given a right of initiative with respect to exchange rates not given to it at Bretton Woods, and it would have to be able to use such initiative in dealing both with excessive creditor countries and with countries falling too heavily in debt. On the other hand, the Americans favored an expanded use of Special Drawing Rights with the aim of making SDRs a true reserve instrument. They saw this as a way of satisfying the numerous members of the Fund that were calling for an expansion of the role of SDRs and, at the same time, as a means of reestablishing a sort of convertibility — at least nominal — for the dollar. They were careful all the same to avoid anything that might threaten the traditional privilege by reason of which the dollar was generally accepted as a reserve currency.

The discussions revolving around these two subjects were prolonged and were finally undercut by events.

The discussions were prolonged because it was not easy to reach agreement on either issue. It became much harder to achieve an accord because the Washington authorities, unhappy about the resistance they met with in the Group of Ten, decided that monetary reform should be fought out in a larger arena with the participation of representatives of third world countries — this forum was the "Group of Twenty." Many governments were disturbed by the idea that the Fund should be given the right to inject itself into their affairs. And it was an almost impossible task to define criteria according to which the Fund should be authorized to propose revaluations or devaluations.

As for elevating SDRs to the status of reserve assets, this not only reawakened some old claims of the third world nations but also posed a delicate problem concerning the respective roles of SDRs and the dollar.

Events conspired to remove all reality from these debates and to provide a convenient way out. The general spread of floating currencies after 1973 forced all countries to recognize that the task of defining a new regime of fixed exchange rates, even rates that could easily be altered, was hardly realistic. It was paradoxical to try to increase the powers of the Fund when so many countries, by floating, in practice avoided its tutelage. After 1974 the enormous increase in dollar reserves, a consequence of the surpluses of the oil-exporting countries, completely undermined the idea of creating still more reserves in the form of SDRs, and the progressive revival of confidence in the dollar provided an additional reason for putting that notion on ice.

Once the old series of discussions was wound up, the negotiations of the Group of Twenty concentrated on trying to decide to what extent floating should be controlled and up to what point each country would have to defend its currency when it came under speculative attack. Above all, it was a question of knowing whether the United States would recognize any obligation to intervene in the case of an unwarranted fall in the value of the dollar. The American representatives became the champions of the thesis according to which their government, while prepared to undertake some limited interventions, did not have to accept any obligation to intervene. The French thesis was the exact opposite. At a meeting of heads of governments held at Rambouillet in November 1975, the question was resolved. It was resolved by resort to ambiguity, thanks to which both the Americans and the French could declare that they had won. It was agreed that the members of the Fund, and the Fund itself, should collaborate "to maintain orderly exchange arrangements and to promote a stable system of exchange rates." But the communiqué was silent as to the means of doing this and as to the responsibilities of various parties. After the Rambouillet meeting the Americans could rightly claim that their policy had not changed — otherwise stated, that they had made no undertaking to support the dollar. For all that, the Rambouillet agreement was interpreted by the market as signaling a new move toward a de facto stabilization of the dollar.

To bring to a conclusion the great negotiation on reform of the international monetary system begun at the end of 1971, nothing remained but to find a suitable way of dressing up an acceptance of the status quo. This was done in Jamaica, in January 1976, by the Interim Committee of the Governors of the International Monetary Fund.

The Jamaica agreement, however, was not wholly devoid of content. It contained precise dispositions on three important points. First, the range of assistance that the Fund was empowered to provide to its members was extended, particularly as far as developing countries are concerned. Second, a new definition of the value of the Special Drawing Right was formulated, which had the effect of ending all connection between the SDR and gold. Finally, some dispositions affecting the yellow metal were made at the insistence of the United States. These are worth careful attention.

During recent years the American government has pursued, and imposed on its partners, systematic action designed to reduce gold to the rank of an ordinary commodity, while at the same time trying to persuade central banks to use it less as a reserve or as a means of settlement. A logical consequence of this view was that central banks should be permitted to dispose of their reserves of metal on the market — a right, as will be recalled, renounced by some of them in March 1968. In November 1973 it was decided that they should be permitted to do this. Furthermore, it followed logically that American citizens should be given the right to hold, buy, and sell gold. This was done in early 1975 — without, it seems, leading to much buying.

It was also considered important to maintain and broaden the March 1968 arrangement under which central banks undertook not to enlarge their gross holdings of gold by purchases on the market. As long as the Bretton Woods agreements had not been formally changed, an ingenious legal interpretation permitted the desired result to be achieved. Although the part of the Articles dealing with exchange parities had been declared dead because of the general floating of currencies, it was ruled that the clauses concerning the price of gold remained in force, despite the great rise in its price on the market. This meant that it was, ipso facto, forbidden to member countries to buy gold on the market where the price was far above the Fund's now purely nominal official price. The amendments to the Articles of Agreement agreed on at Jamaica complicated matters by dropping the clause providing for an official gold price. The United States dealt with this problem by persuading the Group of Ten to agree to abstain, for at least two years, from any action tending either to increase their gross holdings of gold or to stabilize the market price.

This still was not enough. As soon as circumstances permitted, the metal should be discredited; its price should be made to fall, and its future made as uncertain as possible. The best means of doing this would be to sell large amounts from monetary reserves. Since the central banks as a group had traditionally been buyers of several hundred million dollars worth of gold each year, stopping these purchases plus even modest sales ought, it was assumed, to give the market a bad shock. One might have expected the United States to sell substantial quantities from its own gold stock, but it was content with two sales that were little more than symbolic — 23 tons in January 1975 and 16 tons in June of that year. The United States preferred to look to the gold held by the IMF, which arose from the original capital contributions of its members as provided by the Articles, and the supplementary contributions associated with the successive increases in its capital. The Americans managed to get through a decision at the Jamaica Conference whereby one-sixth of the Fund's gold (778 tons) would be sold in parcels from time to time over a period of four years.

Since 1971

It is hard to say to what extent this perseverance has been responsible for the fall in the market price of gold since the beginning of 1975. Fundamentally, it was suspicion about the dollar and about the international monetary system in general that led to a gold price of around $180 per ounce in March 1974 and around $200 per ounce by the end of that year. It is certainly in the renewal of confidence in the dollar and the decline in the rate of inflation throughout the world that the main explanation must be found for the movement that brought the price back down to nearly $100 by the end of 1976. But in 1977 the price climbed again (to around $150 in March). As to whether the effort to demonetize gold will finally attain its objective, it is impossible to judge today.

A Regime Based Increasingly on the Dollar

At the moment the policy we have been describing has turned the monetary gold stock into a dead weight. Obviously, central banks cannot transfer gold among themselves on the basis of the official price ($42.22 per ounce), and experience has proven so far that they do not want to do it on the basis of the market price. Under these conditions it is of little practical importance that they have been authorized to use a price other than the official one, either in their balance sheets (a faculty which only the Bank of France has utilized) or for the purpose of placing a value on quantities of the metal pledged to another central bank (a possibility of which only the Bank of Italy has taken advantage). Since, on the other hand, as we have seen, no more SDRs were created after 1971, the dollar has become the essential cash component in the system. Settlements between central banks are made principally in dollars. The dollar has also remained the instrument used by the monetary authorities in most of their operations on the foreign exchange markets.

On the other hand, the vicissitudes of the American currency have not hindered the continued rapid growth of the Eurocurrency market, favored both by the fact that it responds to a need and by the fact that it escapes all controls. True, the proportion of operations denominated in currencies other than the dollar — particularly in marks — has grown until by the end of 1975 it accounted for around 25 percent of the total. Although the volume of these Eurocurrencies seems to have grown to nearly $200 billion, the monetary authorities have continued to show very little initiative in the presence of the serious problems posed by this phenomenon. They were obliged to take a more active interest in 1974, when it became apparent that various commercial banks had been imprudent. It seems that these imprudences have been largely corrected and that the condition of the market is now healthier.

One new development deserves emphasis. Since the emergence of the large surpluses in the balances of payments of the oil-exporting countries, the amount of monetary reserves invested either directly in the United States or in the Eurodollar market has grown tremendously. In consequence, the deficit countries — European and non-European — have increasingly sought to cover their deficits by borrowing from American banks and on the Eurodollar market. They have seen advantages in this nonpolitical form of debt, which does not necessarily entail conditions about the management of the internal affairs of the borrowing countries. Thus the network of commercial banks of all countries — but mainly the American banks — now performs an increasingly important function in the management of the international monetary system.

In sum, one of the characteristics of the de facto monetary regime under which we live is that its functioning rests to a great degree on dollar mechanisms and circuits and on an international banking structure that carries on its work in dollars. While this regime gives the United States a preponderant role, each country retains its autonomy as to how its exchange rate floats. Order can only be maintained, therefore, at the cost of a minimum of cooperation among the countries responsible for the principal currencies.

Evolving Methods of Cooperation

Between 1971 and 1976 the American attitude toward international monetary cooperation gradually became more flexible.
This is evident even though there was never any formal recog-
nition that a change was occurring.

After August 1971, as we have seen, the U.S. authorities at
first showed little interest in cooperation among the Eleven and
repudiated what had been accomplished up to then within that
framework, especially the network of swap arrangements. They
looked to the developing countries for support in the endeavor
to draft the revised charter they hoped to substitute for
that of Bretton Woods and stimulated the birth of the Committee of Twenty, on which these countries had considerable
weight.

Too large and torn by too many different viewpoints, the Committee of Twenty gradually revealed its powerlessness. And
when the dollar took an alarming dive in 1973, it was the meetings of the Eleven, notably a meeting of the governors of central banks held in Basel in July, which provided the occasion
for the United States to affirm that it was not unconcerned about
the exchange value of its currency. These declarations were
more than platonic, as shown by the fact that the swap agreements revived in 1972 were reinforced in 1973.

The bursting upon the scene of the oil crisis in the autumn
of 1973 and its ramifications weighed in favor of renewed cooperation among the industrial countries. As early as November the new situation was the object of a meeting in France, at
the finance minister level, of the most important countries.
The American proposal for a common energy policy among industrial countries brought the OECD, for which Washington appeared to have little use during the previous period, back to the
center of things. And in 1974 the State Department took the initiative of suggesting a mechanism for mutual financial support
among OECD member countries designed to assure that assis-

tance would be available to those hardest hit by the oil crisis. This was a logical move, and it would have served to reduce, in an opportune fashion, the financial dependence on the oil-exporting countries of those OECD members experiencing the largest deficits. It did constitute, however, a change of attitude, as the Washington authorities had previously always rejected any form of participation in the OECD that would carry with it financial obligations for the United States. One need not be astonished that the State Department's initiative ran into Congressional opposition.

When in 1974 and 1975 the American government moved increasingly toward controlled floating to avoid erratic exchange rate movements, concerted action by the central banks of the Basel Club necessarily became tighter. The concept of collaboration among the Eleven thus gained new ground. And it did so more readily the more the other mechanisms for monetary cooperation proved disappointing. The Fund had no power except to remonstrate insofar as variations in the values of the floating currencies were concerned — a power more theoretical than actual. And the growing weight exercised by the developing countries in its deliberations did not contribute to making the Fund the most appropriate body for the regulation of exchange rate relationships among the industrial countries. As for the cooperation among the countries of the European Economic Community, its decline became more marked year by year. Only the group adhering to the "snake" — unhappily a diminishing group — remained capable of acting as a partner in the international monetary game.

At the end of 1975 and in 1976, a new modality of cooperation made its appearance. At Rambouillet in November 1975 and in Puerto Rico in May 1976, the heads of state of the principal industrial countries themselves chose to discuss monetary problems. The results were not completely negative, at least on the psychological plane. Will this forum prove to be more effective in the future? It is hard to say. But in whatever guise collaboration among the Eleven may be clothed, its return to favor does not seem to be a passing phenomenon. As we shall see, it conforms to the nature of things.

Part Two

LESSONS FROM THE EXPERIENCE – TRUE AND FALSE

The period of monetary history that has unfolded since World War II is rich in what it contains for our instruction. But it is often interpreted in too summary a fashion or in the light of preconceived ideas. This has lent credence to some myths and oversimplifications. Before trying to extract the correct lessons to be drawn from the experience, we must give a fair hearing to some of the myths and oversimplifications.

CHAPTER V

Myths and Oversimplifications

General Condemnation of the Bretton Woods Regime

To judge by some of the pronouncements formulated by persons in high places on both sides of the Atlantic in 1971 and 1972, the postwar monetary system, above all during the 1960s, was defective as such. This general condemnation was enunciated both by some who reproached the system for not being flexible enough and by some who reproached it for not being restrictive enough.

The setbacks recorded and the errors committed during the period 1945-71 should not lead us to fail to recognize the successes achieved, which were considerable. International trade underwent a remarkable growth, encouraged, no doubt, by a large reduction in tariff barriers, but also by a structure of stable and, on the whole, realistic exchange rates. The growth in foreign tourism was prodigious.

Although there was a good deal of inflation throughout the world during the period, it should be recognized that there was hardly any deflation and, at least in industrial countries, relatively little unemployment. Great Britain was the only country that had to curb its economic growth significantly on several

The International Monetary Tangle

occasions for balance of payments reasons, thus registering
a poor growth rate for the period as a whole. This was the result of a number of factors peculiar to Britain, and there is
clearly no justification for holding the international monetary
system responsible. As for the occasional diatribes launched
against the continental European countries for allegedly generating deficits for their trading partners by a reprehensible
style of economic management — one really wonders what they
were getting at. The only creditor country that seems to have
merited serious criticism was Japan, and this particular case
should not be used to support a general conclusion. Even if it
did not engender these two successes — unprecedented growth
of visible and invisible trade and equally unprecedented general
economic growth, marked by only moderate fluctuations in the
growth rate — the Bretton Woods charter had the great merit
of making them possible.

We must recognize the negative aspects of the regime. It is
reasonable to ask to what extent it was responsible for worldwide inflation as well as for the disorderly growth of a mass
of liquid assets whose movement from place to place led to
trouble and an atmosphere of insecurity. We must note that
some large countries recorded a chronic deficit in their balances of payments. We will return to these matters. But, to
begin with, we should discard the thesis that the system failed
on balance.

A more moderate thesis is that although the Bretton Woods
regime rendered good service, corresponding to the needs of a
certain epoch, that epoch is over. A wholly new situation has
been created, it might be argued, with which the 1944 charter
cannot cope because some of its provisions are not, or are no
longer, suitable.

Today the Bretton Woods agreements are buried and there is
little chance that they will be revived. But it is by no means a
waste of time to examine, in the light of what has transpired
both before and since 1971, the validity of the criticisms directed at those agreements on certain points.

Myths and Oversimplifications

The Alleged Responsibility of Gold

One criticism is directed at the role allotted to gold in the 1944 charter. It is not reasonable, people say, that the smooth working of the international monetary system should be compromised by developments in the free gold market which is, after all, only a market for a metal and like any other such market subject to speculative influences.

This criticism overlooks the fact that the reasons why in March 1968 the central banks had to give up trying to make the official price prevail on the market were that the short-term foreign debt of the United States had reached such figures that there was growing doubt as to the possibility of maintaining the convertibility into gold of the dollars they held, and that a huge mass of dollars was being thrown onto the market for conversion into gold. The growth of the short-term debt of the United States, in turn, was explainable by the fact that the United States made excessive use of the facilities of the gold exchange standard to cover its balance of payments deficits.

Opinions differ as to what the Americans ought to have done. Should they not long ago have eliminated their deficit by reforming their policies? Should their European and Japanese partners not have helped reduce the deficit by giving them meaningful concessions, particularly on trade? Should the Americans not have restricted capital exports more than they did? Should they not have surmounted their repugnance toward asking for assistance and done as most other countries in deficit did, by seeking support from the resources of the International Monetary Fund or other borrowed resources? We shall return to the discussion of these points and will make the case that it would have been wise to finance part of the U.S. deficit by resort to long- and medium-term credits from Western Europe and Japan.

The fact remains that the progressive creation of short-term liabilities in dollars several times greater than the size of the American gold reserve could not fail to end in disaster, notably by making any equilibrium in the gold market impossible.

But the drafters of the Bretton Woods charter, it is sometimes said, were at fault not to foresee that gold was not well
suited to provide an adequate supply of reserves, given the high
level of foreign exchange resources that countries taken together desired to hold; in a future monetary regime it would
be better to have a new fiduciary reserve instrument to make
up for the inadequacy of gold and ultimately to replace it. Those
who make this argument forget that there was a clause in the
Articles of Agreement of the IMF providing for an agreed general increase in the price of gold. It was above all the United
States that opposed activating this procedure, thus preventing
what would have been an entirely warranted upward adjustment
of the price. It is also forgotten that the Bretton Woods agreements did not pretend to have solved all monetary problems.
The drafters did not exclude complementary arrangements
among members whereby some of them could open lines of
credit capable of alleviating the pressure on gold reserves. It
is not the fault of the charter that what has been done along this
line up to now has been inadequate.

It is somewhat dishonest, therefore, to claim that the pre-
1971 experience demonstrated the need to revise the concept
that prevailed at Bretton Woods concerning gold as a reserve
instrument.

But, add the adversaries of the precious metal, events since
1971 confirm that from now on gold is unsuited to fill the monetary role assigned to it (probably wrongly) in the past. How is
it possible, they ask, to rely for the reserves of central banks
on a commodity whose price bounded from below $45 per ounce
at the end of 1971 to nearly $200 by the end of 1974 and then
fell in eighteen months to around $100 per ounce? These enor-
mous fluctuations are a force for either inflation or deflation
in the system, and in any case a cause of disorder and instability.

It is too easily forgotten that these regrettable ups and downs
of the gold price were largely the product — sometimes intended and sometimes not intended — of the policies of the monetary authorities themselves, especially those of the United

Myths and Oversimplifications

States. The rise in 1972, 1973, and 1974 reflected a general
mistrust of currencies — especially the dollar, long proclaimed
to be inconvertible — and mistrust of the whole international
monetary system. As soon as inflation abated and a certain order seemed to be established in exchange parities, it was natural that the gold price should fall from the exceptionally high
level it had reached. But it was not at all natural that, at the
same time, a systematic American policy should precipitate
and aggravate this fall. By arbitrarily preventing central banks
from buying gold and obliging the market, whose function it is
to supply monetary gold, to absorb it, the United States succeeded in increasing the instability of the metal. This instability proves that, at least temporarily, U.S. policy worked. It
cannot be used to demonstrate that the policy was right.

We shall return to the problem of gold, its qualities and its
defects. For the moment we must simply note that nothing in
the postwar experience indicates a need for terminating the
monetary role of gold. It is, by the way, a much older experience that is often invoked as a motive for the crusade against
gold. It is held that the fetish that surrounds the precious
metal was one of the causes of the great crisis of the 1930s.
This is not the place to discuss that claim, except to suggest
that even if it is valid as concerns the use of gold as a unit of
account, it is not valid with regard to the use of gold as a component of reserves and as a means of payment. For the moment we rest with the conclusion that since World War II the
disorders in the gold market have been the effects, not the
causes, of international monetary disorder.

The Sins of the "Extreme Creditors"

What validity is there to the claim that one of the main dis-
equilibrating factors from which the Bretton Woods regime suffered was the policies followed by the "extreme creditors," and
that consequently one of the principal reforms for the future
must be to reinforce the means of pressure that can be used in

dealing with such countries? In this train of thought there is
some truth, but also some exaggeration and a number of de-
batable propositions.

Let us begin by examining who were the "extreme creditors"
up to 1971, how they behaved, and what may have been the
wrongs they did to the international community as a whole.

At the end of the war and during the immediately following
years, the United States was the big "extreme creditor." This
was a consequence both of the immense economic strength of
the United States in a war-weakened world and of the stability
of American prices at a time when inflation was widespread
elsewhere. Conscious of its responsibilities and also desirous
of avoiding an application to the dollar of the "scarce currency"
clause of the Fund Articles, the United States, by loans and
grants, liberally financed the rest of the world's deficits up to
the time when the recovery of Western Europe and Japan led
to the disappearance of the surplus in the American balance of
payments. With the single exception of some aspects of its
tariff policy that might be criticized, the United States conducted itself as an exemplary "extreme creditor."

Shortly after the war it became apparent that Belgium posed
for its European partners the problems of an "extreme creditor." This occurred because Belgium followed a stricter internal economic policy than did the other members of the OEEC.
Its partners in the OEEC, however, could charge that Belgium
was perhaps sacrificing too much in the way of large public
works to considerations of monetary and financial orthodoxy.
However that may have been, the Belgian case was debated at
length and frequently, both within the OEEC, in the European
Payments Union, and before European public opinion. Belgium
granted large credits to its partners. And the problem itself
disappeared as soon as the differences between the policies of
Belgium and those of most other Western European countries
faded. Not only was Belgium not an obstacle to European economic recovery, it acted as a useful brake on the tendency of
some countries to be too lax.

Even before 1960 and throughout the decade of the 1960s, the

Myths and Oversimplifications

Federal Republic of Germany was the star "extreme creditor," first on the European scale and later on the world scale. That was the result, above all, of the remarkable stability of the purchasing power of the mark. In general the Federal Republic conducted itself as a cooperative creditor. It cannot be reproached for having curbed either merchandise imports or capital exports. On the whole it followed a policy of growth and full employment. It granted large financial facilities in the framework of the European Payments Union, in that of the International Monetary Fund and the World Bank, as well as in the form of bilateral agreements with the United States and Great Britain. It accumulated enormous dollar holdings without asking the United States for gold. Several times it raised the value of its currency in relation to the dollar to a degree that imposed a difficult task on its export industries. The only reproach that might in fairness be made is that the Federal Republic relied too much on monetary policy, in preference to other methods, to resist price increases, thus attracting liquid assets from abroad. But one cannot honestly hold it responsible for the difficulties experienced by France prior to 1958, nor for those of the United States after 1960, nor for the chronic troubles that affected Britain for thirty years.

There remains the case of the last of the "extreme creditors" — Japan. Here it must be recognized that several aspects of Japanese policy deserved to be regarded as subject to criticism by the rest of the international community. But it must be added that Japan did accumulate enormous amounts of dollars without asking for their conversion to gold. In any event, while one might reproach Japan for contributing excessively to the deterioration in balance of trade of the United States and of some European countries, it cannot be held responsible for the troubles of the international monetary system.

Apart, then, from the case of Japan, the record of the "extreme creditors," especially that of the United States when it was in that position, is much better than seems to be generally supposed. If this is so, it is probably to some extent because, contrary to the conventional wisdom, the "extreme creditors" were in fact subjected to considerable pressure.

When the United States was an "extreme creditor" immediately after the war, it had of its own accord a high sense of its duty toward the rest of the world, particularly toward Europe. But Belgium, the Federal Republic of Germany, and Japan were all placed in the position of indicted parties. No doubt the Articles of Agreements of the Monetary Fund dealt in a rather summary fashion with the responsibilities of creditors. That must not be taken as a basis for concluding that the management of the Fund, especially Per Jacobsson and Pierre Paul Schweitzer, remained passive and failed to use their authority unofficially to bring about the desired cooperation of the creditors. It must not be overlooked either that in the OEEC, in the Management Committee of the European Payments Union, as well as in the OECD and the Group of Ten, the creditor countries were placed on the stand, their policies were put through the sieve and discussed, and even in the absence of material pressures, they were exposed to moral pressures the force of which should not be underestimated. Finally, both with Bonn and with Tokyo the American government used, or at least implied that it might use, various means of pressure that were at its command.

Since mid-1971 the problem of "extreme creditors" has acquired a new dimension. On the one hand, Switzerland has joined the cohort of sinners, consisting essentially of the countries of the "snake," the Swiss Confederation, and at times Japan. On the other hand, the floating of currencies has put the creditor countries in a very uncomfortable position. Because speculators tended to push their currencies up, they had the option of buying amounts of inconvertible dollars that could become enormous or of letting their currencies appreciate, which penalized their exporters. This is what has moved the Swiss franc and the mark by stages to unreasonably high levels. And one cannot be sure that in several cases this speculation was not stimulated by rumors spread in the debtor countries.

This mechanism has proved so effective in weakening the

competitive position of the "extreme creditors" and in easing the position of the dollar that the United States willingly abandoned the other weapon it was brandishing against the "extreme creditors," namely, a change in the Articles of Agreement enabling the Fund to punish those countries by forcing them to change their policies, perhaps even their exchange rates. This project foundered in 1975 along with the rest of the plan for revising the articles.

Confronted by this policy, which caught them in a painful dilemma, the creditor countries showed remarkable patience. They would have been morally justified in having recourse to some defensive action. They could have protected their economies by surtaxes on imports and by export bonuses. Inspired by the system adopted by Belgium many years ago, they could have established a double exchange market designed to permit commercial operations to continue to be carried out at an acceptable rate of exchange. For various reasons they did none of these things.[8] And as a group (Japan once again being the only exception) they gave no grounds for their partners to reproach them for their import policies.

Altogether, the case against the "extreme creditors" looks fragile. What is more, one wonders if it does not rest on faulty concepts.

The notion that there is a symmetry between the obligations of creditor countries and those of debtor countries has a certain polish to it. Just as debtor countries must reduce their rates of inflation, creditor countries should increase theirs. Rates of inflation being more or less harmonized thanks to the coordination of domestic policies, rates of exchange should become relatively stable. Unfortunately, such an idea is utterly utopian.

When all countries are sliding down the slope of inflation,

---

8. Except that France established a double exchange market in 1971 and dropped it in 1974.

with rates of increase in the cost of living over five percent and sometimes around ten, it would require some sort of miracle for them to manage to equalize their rates of inflation. Once prices and wages start chasing each other upward, all that can be done is to try to slow them down as much as possible; but it is impossible to control the movements with any precision. The experience of the 1971-76 period is revealing in this respect. There was inflation almost everywhere, but almost always at different rates in different countries. Even within the small group of the "snake," reduced to the Federal Republic of Germany and a few other countries within which efforts at harmonizing policies were made, disparities between the rates of depreciation in the purchasing power of money persisted, posing difficult problems for the group's survival. It is certainly true that an adequate degree of equalization of rates of inflation is a condition for stability in exchange relationships. But this equalization can only be achieved if the rates of inflation are not much above zero.

Creditor countries do indeed have obligations. They ought to be liberal toward commodity imports and toward capital exports. It is normal for them to extend credit to their partners whose balances of payments are in deficit and whose currencies are vulnerable. But they must not be asked to let their prices rise.

In other words, it is a mistake to consider the problem of creditor countries too much from the point of view of the difficulties experienced by the debtor countries and their desire for relief. Worldwide inflation must be considered, and the role that the international monetary system ought to play in curbing inflationary tendencies. It is, in fact, a good thing that all countries do not permit themselves to go at the same speed along the easy route. The fact that some countries go more slowly ought naturally to have a certain moderating influence on the whole international community. For this influence to be felt, creditor countries must not be required to submit to dictates inspired by the debtor countries.

Myths and Oversimplifications

Good and Bad Use of the Gold Exchange Standard

From another quarter altogether, a school of liberal economists in recent years has condemned the practice of the gold
exchange standard, that is, the practice whereby central banks
hold part of their reserves in foreign exchange. The principal
spokesman for this group, M. Jacques Rueff, has proposed that an
international agreement to outlaw this technique be adopted.

What does the history of this last third of a century teach us
about this matter? We can say immediately that it suggests a
qualified judgment. It is not the gold exchange standard as such
that is revealed to be pernicious, but rather the way in which
it was abused, mainly for the benefit of the United States.

There is nothing abnormal about the holding of sterling as
reserves by the members of the sterling area, of dollars by
the developing countries within the U.S. orbit, or of francs by
the countries in the franc area. The collaboration thus established between a country with a money and capital market and
a number of developing countries to which it furnishes aid, and
with which it has traditional ties, is advantageous for the countries so assisted. The amounts of foreign exchange those countries are able to accumulate are not likely, apart from exceptional circumstances, to be important for long on the world
scale. When it is not accompanied by unfair trade discrimination, this practice holds no dangers for the international community.

In the same way, when some oil-exporting countries began to
accumulate enormous cash balances after the autumn of 1973,
which they obviously could not use for a long time, most of
them in dollars and some in sterling, the practice proved satisfactory on the whole for all parties concerned. It is true that
in the spring of 1976, when the pound was badly shaken, some
of the deposits were withdrawn from London, thus contributing
to sterling's fall.

By contrast, as we have seen, it was a disaster for the international community when during the 1960s the short-term

external dollar debt of the United States gradually rose to figures that could not fail to shatter confidence in the convertibility of the dollar and in the stability of its exchange value.

In passing, we must remove a misunderstanding about the responsibility in this matter sometimes attributed to the Bretton Woods charter. The Articles of the Monetary Fund imposed no obligation whatever on a member country to hold the currency of another country in its reserves without asking for its conversion. A member country was, of course, not prohibited from holding the currency of another country. It was however contrary to the spirit of the Articles that a deficit country should systematically finance its deficit by a method that enabled it to avoid both the discipline that results from a loss of reserves and that which results from the necessity of calling on external assistance — a method that provided it with the means to live for too long in a state of disequilibrium. It was no less contrary to the spirit of the Articles to proceed in a manner that resulted in making the convertibility of currencies impossible. The abuses of the gold exchange standard that occurred in the years up to 1971 were not consistent with the spirit of Bretton Woods.

Was this accumulation of dollars not bound to be fatal, given the size and persistence of the deficit in the American balance of payments? Not at all. The creditor countries had very good reasons for giving credit to the United States and for not demanding gold settlement of their claims. But there were possible forms of credit other than the accumulation of short-term dollar assets and not having the same drawbacks.

After 1971 the countries that continued to buy large amounts of dollars (mainly the Federal Republic of Germany and Switzerland) did so in order to avoid an excessive appreciation of their currencies and an excessive depreciation of the American currency. The aim was laudable, and we have seen how, as time went on, the need to exert more control over floating rates became more and more imperative. But the technique employed was clearly not the best possible.

Myths and Oversimplifications

The United States left it mostly up to other countries to support the dollar. This necessarily left it uncertain whether those countries would be disposed to accumulate sufficiently large holdings of inconvertible foreign exchange assets whose value to them was not guaranteed. Speculators felt encouraged. The situation would have been different if more use had been made of another technique, namely, defense by the United States itself of the value of its currency, using foreign exchange resources borrowed from its partners.

We are thus led to conclude that it was an error before as well as after 1971 to rely to an excessive degree on the methods of the gold exchange standard to deal with problems that could have been resolved better by other means.

Essentially, this error can be charged against the United States, which always disliked contracting external debts denominated in anything but dollars and for whom the gold exchange standard furnished an ideal means of going into debt without appearing to do so. Some part of the fault lay also with Western Europe and Japan, which during the 1960s acquiesced too complacently in continuing to finance the American deficit by unhealthy means. Although the rest of the international community suffered the consequences of this policy, it bore none of the responsibility for it. Moreover, until 1973 the central banks outside the industrial countries rarely accumulated durable reserves of any significant size. The situation in which the oil-exporting countries found themselves after 1973 was exceptional, perhaps a one-time occurrence. In any case, the growth of their dollar reserves has been fortunate both for them and for international monetary equilibrium.

We may conclude that an unqualified condemnation of the gold exchange standard seems to be unwarranted, that on the other hand the accumulation of excessive amounts of dollars by the industrial countries over a period of fifteen years was a regrettable phenomenon, and that the United States was granted credits to too great an extent through the mechanism of the gold exchange standard and not often enough by the use of other

The International Monetary Tangle

methods that would not have had the same disadvantages. There is matter here for serious reflection concerning the future, to which we will return in detail below.

The Rigidity of Parities under the Bretton Woods Regime

It is often claimed that the Bretton Woods regime placed obstacles in the way of speedy changes in parities, either up or down, which the situation might call for — or at any rate did not sufficiently favor them. Changes often having been decided on too late, it is said, they did not yield all the expected beneficial results.

One of the clearest cases of an adjustment delayed too long was the devaluation of the French franc carried out in 1958 (or, rather, carried out in two steps in 1957 and 1958). But it was a brilliant success. True, it was accompanied by the adoption of a solid program of correcting imbalances in the domestic economy. The devaluation of the pound in 1967 should probably have been decided on when the Labour Government came to power in 1964. It did not, at least at once, have the hoped for happy consequences. It did so eventually, and it is evident that the good results were achieved as soon as various corrective measures were applied to the domestic economy. As for the mark, it is frequently held that its second upward revaluation, in 1969, came too late and therefore missed its target. To which it must be replied that a very convincing explanation of the feeble effect of this revaluation on the size of the West German surplus is that the change of parity was not accompanied by a change in the underlying causes of the surplus, which were to be found largely outside the Federal Republic.[9] The clearest lesson from the past in these matters is that changes in exchange rates not accompanied by a policy capable of

9. In addition, when the West German government revalued the mark on various occasions, it did so largely to reinforce its anti-inflation policy.

eliminating the causes of disequilibrium in the balance of payments run a strong risk of proving powerless to reestablish
any durable equilibrium. We must therefore not exaggerate the
consequences of deferring certain parity changes for too long
or seek to explain by these delays setbacks that were actually
due to other causes.

It remains true that during the years before 1971, governments often waited until too late to make necessary adjustments
in exchange rates. Should the International Monetary Fund be
held responsible for this? That would be highly unjust.

Legally, according to the Bretton Woods agreements, the initiative for changes in parity rested with the governments concerned, while the role of the Fund was to decide on such proposed changes as might be submitted to it. Apparently, the Fund
has never refused to approve a proposal for a change that has
been laid before it. It has even given its stamp of approval to
some devaluations that might be considered excessive. Furthermore, at the very beginning of its existence, the Fund cleared
away any possible misunderstanding as to its doctrine. "The
Fund Agreement makes it clear," says the 1948 annual report,
"that the provisions for the regulation of exchange rates are
not intended to impose on the Fund the duty of perpetuating in
the name of stability exchange rates that have lost touch with
economic realities. Stability and rigidity are different concepts."

As a practical matter, the Articles of Agreement did not de-
ter Per Jacobsson and P. P. Schweitzer from using unofficial
pressure on several countries to induce them to change their
parities. They found it proper for them to do this whenever the
maintenance of the existing parity inevitably entailed practices
on the legitimacy of which the Fund did have authority to pronounce. There is every reason to believe that both of them
made as extensive use as possible of the authority they disposed of. There is also every reason to believe that their influence was often important in persuading governments to make
changes about which they were having difficulty in making up
their minds. In particular, Per Jacobsson applied his talent

The International Monetary Tangle

and his prestige in 1957 and 1958 to make the French leadership understand the necessity for a devaluation of the franc.

Furthermore, the most striking case of an exchange rate adjustment that was too long deferred is probably that of the dollar. It is clear, from today's vantage point, that it would have been better not to wait until 1971 to devalue it. No less striking, though more controversial, is the case of gold whose official price, it seems reasonable to believe, should have been increased, or abandoned, long before 1976. In neither of these cases is there any basis for blaming the drafters of the Articles of Agreement of the Monetary Fund. It was not their fault that the American Congress, when ratifying the Articles, adopted a law that, as we have seen, made the price of gold and the parity of the dollar sacrosanct.

The myth that holds that the Bretton Woods regime was a factor in the excessive rigidity of exchange parities is, to some extent, at the source of the proposal, advanced by the United States after 1971, under which the Fund would be given the power in certain hypothetical situations to recommend changes in exchange rates on its own initiative. As the project for drawing up a new charter has been abandoned, any debate on that proposal has become academic. It is not, however, without interest to reflect on what might have happened in the past if the Fund had been endowed from the beginning with the right to take the initiative on exchange rate matters.

It seems highly unlikely that the Fund would have had the nerve to raise officially the question of a devaluation of sterling in 1947, 1948, or at the beginning of 1949. It was unthinkable before 1971 that it would dare to question the parity of the dollar. By contrast, it doubtless would have been led to take up the problem of the French franc in the period prior to December 1958. Can anyone imagine that this would have made General de Gaulle any better disposed to make the decision that he finally made? If Mr. Jacobsson and M. Schweitzer were able to act effectively in dealing with various countries, it was precisely because their interventions preserved a personal and

Myths and Oversimplifications

confidential character and were made with the necessary tact. The truth is that a change in parity is a vital decision for a nation, which can affect the level of consumption and employment of every citizen. It would be psychologically impossible for such a decision to be made by any authority other than the government of that nation. If the Fund had been given the authority to suggest parity changes, even without the right to impose them, an undesirable situation would have prevailed. There are no secrets in such matters. It is enough that a change should be considered and studied for part of its effect to be realized by anticipation, thus creating a fait accompli. The confidential relationships that grew up over the years between the Fund and its principal members could not have been the same. The ostensible privilege granted to the Fund would, in reality, have been a poisoned gift.

*   *   *

At this stage in our reflections, it appears that although the international monetary system may have worked poorly during the 1960s, it is not right to conclude too quickly that its foundations were unsound. The Bretton Woods charter should not be made responsible for the mistakes of management that were committed, above all when those mistakes were in violation of the Articles of Agreement. Governments and the governed are always tempted to look for scapegoats for the consequences of their failures. With this in mind, the accusations against gold and against the creditor countries must be treated circumspectly. Account must also be taken of all sorts of imponderable factors. That some fruitful actions were taken unofficially, sometimes outside the framework of the Fund, sometimes in verbal and confidential form, does not mean that they were not done and done well. We shall therefore endeavor in the following chapters to guard against too much simplification and too much generalization. We shall try, rather, to draw the lessons of experience concerning particular problems — without forgetting that circumstances diverge widely throughout the world and that the same principles are not necessarily applicable to all currencies.

CHAPTER VI

The Quarrel over Floating Exchange Rates

Fixed exchange rates and floating exchange rates are often presented as opposites. Actually, there are not two but three options: fixed rates, freely floating rates, and controlled floating. The formula of free floating (baptized by its apostles as "clean floating," as opposed to "dirty floating," which is how they regard controlled floating) was defended by the American authorities for a short time after August 1971. As we have already noted, they were led to move farther and farther away from that position, and no other government adopted it. In fact, the theory of free floating is nothing but an intellectual game. What experience teaches us about controlled floating, by contrast, is both far from being negative and far from being simple.

Before considering the lessons of the post-1971 period, it is of interest to remind ourselves of what took place in the way of floating exchange rates under the Bretton Woods regime. The Fund did not dissuade France from adopting a floating rate from 1948 to 1958. It authorized Canada to float its dollar from 1950 to 1962 and again after 1970.

The floating of the franc in 1948 was a useful expedient that enabled the French government to obtain public acceptance of a necessary devaluation. But it quickly became apparent that under a regime of exchange controls, the behavior of the market depended primarily on decisions of the authorities and was not determined by the free play of natural forces. The franc soon became the object of a de facto stabilization at a level that could not subsequently be abandoned without a decision on the part of authorities that was, psychologically and politically, very much like a decision to devalue. When, after 1952, a slipping of the rate began to become necessary, the government thought for several years that it need not make up its mind on the matter. The status of being a floating currency did not preclude prolonged maintenance of the franc at a level that was too ambitious.

Canada is a special case because of the predominant role in its balance of payments of its relations with the United States, especially American investments in Canada and Canadian borrowings on the New York market. The floating of the Canadian dollar has always been controlled and kept within quite narrow limits.

The detractors of the Fund easily forget that it did not maintain an intransigent attitude on these matters. It would certainly not have discouraged the United States from making an experiment in floating after 1971 if the United States had chosen to seek its authorization.

That said, what lessons may we draw from the experiment of general floating undertaken after 1971?

We should first recall that this floating has practically always been a controlled floating, the degree of control varying at different periods and for different currencies. Except for the United States, all the industrial countries have intervened substantially in the market to buy or sell exchange. And while the American authorities have done little of this, the other countries have in a sense replaced them by buying dollars, sometimes in enormous amounts, in an attempt to limit the depreciation of that currency. It is not always easy today to distinguish, among the good and bad features of our present regime, what is due to the fact that it is one of floating and what to the fact that it is one of controlled, or "dirty," floating.

The International Monetary Tangle

On the other hand, if there was ever a period in which floating commended itself even to those who dislike it a priori and
fear the consequences, it is certainly the period from 1971 to
the present. Unprecedented inflation, strong fluctuations in
economic activity throughout the world in 1973, 1974, and 1975,
increases of 300 to 400 percent in oil prices — all these events
and their repercussions made frequent adjustments in exchange
rates inevitable. Recourse to floating was justified, at least
for a transitory period.

One of the objections to floating was the fear that exchange
instability would put a brake on the growth of international
trade. This fear has not materialized up to now, at least not
to any marked extent. Probably some small or medium-sized
firms have been discouraged by the complications and the new
risks involved in exporting. But as a whole, commercial enter-
prises and the banks have adapted remarkably well; most of the
time they have found the means of resolving the technical problems presented by fluctuating rates.

This remark leads to another concerning the effect of the depreciation and appreciation of currencies on trade balances.
The countries whose currencies have been revalued upward in
successive stages (mainly the mark and the Swiss franc) have
been able to limit to a surprising extent adverse effects on their
foreign trade. Generally, after a comparatively short time a
favorable, or at least acceptable, position has been reestablished. It is true that these countries have never ceased to apply a rather strict anti-inflationary policy internally. As for the
countries whose currencies have depreciated (the United States,
Great Britain, Italy), the consequences seem to have depended
largely on the domestic policies followed. At first the depreciation of the dollar that took place between August 1971 and July
1973 brought no noticeable improvement in the American balance of trade. But in 1971-72 monetary expansion was in vogue
in the United States. The turnaround in the trade balance more
or less coincided with the activation of a policy of monetary
stringency. As for the disappointing results of the deep devaluations of the pound and the lira, it is hard to refrain from

relating them to the high rates of inflation that prevailed in the countries concerned.

This lesson from the post-1971 experience confirms the lesson we drew from the previous period. Whatever the rate of exchange, there can be no external equilibrium if there is no internal equilibrium. To say that if there is internal equilibrium, there would be external equilibrium no matter what the rate of exchange would go too far. The rate of exchange is important: a rate that is too unfavorable can constitute an almost insurmountable obstacle. But it seems that there is a tendency to exaggerate the importance of the rate. A parity that might be considered somewhat overvalued, judging by calculations of comparative prices, does not, ipso facto, need to be changed.

On the whole, we are led to conclude that the export capacity of a country is not affected as much as has often been supposed by an imperfect exchange rate, whether it is too high or simply not very stable. The determining factors are the degree of equilibrium in the domestic economy and the technical capacities of the country's industries.

Floating, nonetheless, has serious disadvantages in other respects if it is not adequately controlled. We have witnessed the development of irrational and speculative movements of funds leading to large oscillations, both up and down. Thus the value of the Swiss franc in terms of dollars increased by more than 20 percent from May to July 1973, fell by more than 21 percent by January 1974, rose by 19 percent by May 1974, fell again by nearly 5 percent between May and September 1974, then climbed more than 25 percent by February 1975, only to drop again more than 11 percent by July 1975. Such fluctuations in both directions during such a short period were clearly not warranted by corresponding changes in the purchasing powers of the two currencies. They created difficult problems for those who had to manage cash or draw up accounts. They exposed banks and corporate treasurers to temptations to speculate that they did not always resist. Such fluctuations contributed to the spread of a general sense of insecurity — a distrust of all currencies. It must be because they became aware of these dangers that the

U. S. authorities moved progressively toward a stricter control of the exchange market.

One thing the men of Bretton Woods greatly feared was competitive devaluations and the chain reaction they were likely to set off. Recent experience has not so far been very conclusive on this point. The first excessive devaluation was that of the dollar in 1973. But against a partner as powerful as the United States, nobody could seriously consider retaliation. The recent depreciation of the pound and the lira has obviously gone beyond what was required from the point of view of the competitive position of either Britain or Italy. But given the pace of inflation in both countries, their partners had no reason to be too uneasy. (French farmers, however, got special measures adopted to protect them against imports of Italian origin.) Japan's case was somewhat more delicate, as it was accused in 1976 of intervening in the market to maintain too favorable a rate for the yen and at the same time curbing imports. We should also mention that the regime of generalized floating did not facilitate progress in the trade negotiations within the framework of GATT, known as the "Tokyo Round," designed to bring about a new batch of tariff reductions.

Another eventuality feared by the men of Bretton Woods has probably come to pass: they feared that some countries, by being able to devalue their currencies without hindrance, would let themselves slide too easily along the slope of inflation. If Britain and Italy from 1972 on and France from 1976 on had found themselves under the tutelage of the Fund with respect to their exchange rates and obliged to obtain its approval for their actions, there is reason to believe that this might have been a salutary restraint. In France in July 1976, while the franc was slipping by about 10 percent on the market, the Finance Minister assured the French people that the government would not devalue the currency; in a sense, he spoke the truth.

As we have seen above, floating also served to increase the gap between countries that kept better control over their domestic inflation and those that did less well. Some upward revaluations made possible by the floating helped those in the first group to contain price increases. Some devaluations, also aided by the floating, helped those in the second group to persist in their lax policies and, as a result of the increase in the prices of their imports, stimulated the general rise in prices.

But the ground gained against inflation in the first group of countries was, we fear, less than that lost in the second group. In other words, it is to be feared that inflation has been on the winning side.

Must one finally prefer a system like that of Bretton Woods as a permanent regime? Or would a system of controlled floating be better? Some hesitation is permissible. We believe that the lessons of the whole period from 1946 to 1976 tend to support the first alternative, provided that, in exceptional circumstances, resort to floating is expressly permitted.

All this debate has a somewhat academic character today. A regime of controlled floating prevails whose adoption was justified by an extraordinary situation. It is not about to come to an end. The real problem today is to know under what conditions it can work properly. To this problem the following pages will be devoted.

CHAPTER VII

Methods of International Monetary Cooperation

From the history of these past thirty years one important lesson seems to stand out.

It is essential to complement the nearly worldwide system of cooperation, of which the International Monetary Fund is the center, by some form of special collaboration among certain countries that must involve both a coordination of their policies and mutual financial support. The countries concerned are those between which short- and long-term capital movements give rise to problems of a particular size and nature that are super-imposed on the problems all countries have by reason of fluctuations in their current balances of payments. Let us say that there are about eleven such countries, and let us label them "financial market countries." [10]

Ever since World War II these countries have pirouetted around this problem, sometimes coming up with apparently satisfactory solutions, but solutions that proved to be precarious, and finally proving incapable not only of solving the

---

10. To remind: the "Group of Ten" includes eleven members: the United States, Great Britain, seven continental European countries, Canada, and Japan.

problems but even of becoming fully aware of their nature. The monetary history of the period since the Bretton Woods Conference consists in part of these tentative efforts, partial successes, and this setback.

It will be recalled that the very year after the Conference the Anglo-American Agreement of December 1945 endeavored to reestablish the convertibility of sterling through a bilateral convention accompanied by a loan to Britain approved by the U. S. Congress. Soon thereafter intimate financial cooperation between the United States and Western Europe was established in the OEEC, and the European countries' deficits were covered by a series of grants and loans from the American government. It would have been impossible to ask the Fund to meet such large requirements, and the World Bank itself soon reduced its lending to Europe to a few countries in special situations in order to devote itself almost completely to the developing countries. Shortly after the Marshall Plan was activated, the need arose for some arrangements to rejuvenate intra-European trade and financial relations. These arrangements developed into the European Payments Union. It should be emphasized that although these accomplishments took place outside the formal structure of the IMF, they were done in liaison with it, were carried out with a careful eye to remaining in harmony with the Fund's objectives, and resulted in placing the countries of Western Europe in a position to conform to the Bretton Woods agreements by making their currencies convertible. What was done outside the Fund was indispensable if the Fund was to be enabled to function properly.

We have noted that after the move to convertibility of the principal European currencies, the illusion that there was no further need for a collaboration sui generis between North America and Western Europe was short-lived. To deal with the problems that arose between them, and between them and Japan, all sorts of new moves were called for. This led to the renewal of activity by the BIS and the zeal of the Americans in the Basel meetings after about 1960. Then came the creation of the OECD in 1961. The General Arrangements to Borrow and

the establishment of the Group of Ten followed at the end of
1961. Then came the organization of the "gold pool" in 1962.
This was followed by the various arrangements — written or
verbal, explicit or tacit — designed to make the Europeans and
the Japanese finance as much as possible of the American deficit (prepayments of debts, subscriptions to "Roosa bonds,"
and above all, the accumulation of dollar balances by the monetary authorities and the banks). The American deficit vis-à-vis
Europe and Japan in the period that began in 1958, like the European deficit vis-à-vis the United States in the immediate postwar period, was not covered to any important degree by the
Monetary Fund. And if this whole sequence of events ended in
a fiasco, it was not because it would have been unhealthy to finance part of the American deficit by European and Japanese
assistance. On the contrary, it would have been entirely acceptable to extend loans to the United States, the more so because
from 1958 to at least 1971 the net increase in U. S. foreign assets seems to have been greater than the whole of the deficits
in its balance of payments. Things turned out badly because the
accumulation of a growing mass of short-term liabilities was
a bad financial practice that could only end in a crisis of confidence.

Finally, we should recall that after the suspension of dollar
convertibility, the position of the United States with respect to
cooperation among the Eleven, or within the OECD, began again
to fluctuate. At the beginning of the period the United States
showed its dislike of this formula. Then, under the pressure
of events, it withdrew bit by bit from its negative attitude. It
became obvious, in particular, that the necessary surveillance
of the foreign exchange markets presupposed some concerted
action by the monetary authorities of several countries. But
although the change in the American attitude was quite marked,
it has not yet been clearly enunciated. The methods of cooperation among the Eleven have remained imprecise and empirical.
The results have nevertheless been good.

Let us forget history for a moment and reflect on the nature of the problems that international capital movements pose for balances of payments and, eventually, exchange rates, and also on the kinds of solutions that these problems call for.

As a matter of fact, short-term capital only moves between a small number of countries: the United States, Great Britain, the seven continental European countries having a money market in the proper sense of the term (Belgium, France, the Federal Republic of Germany, Italy, the Netherlands, Sweden, Switzerland), Canada, and Japan — that is, eleven countries altogether. No doubt a few other market centers may be affected by great international movements of liquid assets, but they are affected only marginally and any effects on them are limited. No doubt other countries, including developing countries, are also familiar with the phenomenon of short-term capital movements. But on the one hand, they have practically no acquaintance with massive arrivals of liquid assets from abroad, and on the other hand, the outflows of capital from which they sometimes suffer affect mainly assets owned by their nationals and raise no problems basically different from those posed by a disequilibrium in the balance of payments on current account.

By contrast, for the eleven countries considered short-term capital movements — not always connected with a disequilibrium in either the balance of trade or the balance on current account as a whole — constitute a phenomenon sui generis, both in its size and in its nature. In any case, given the volume of liquid holdings capable of being moved from one market to another, especially those held by the large multinational corporations, the resources that have been mobilized to compensate for fluctuations in current account balances are inadequate to cope with the consequences of such migrations for the exchange reserves of the countries involved.

It is not only supplementary resources to finance this phenomenon that are called for. Short-term capital movements depend to a large extent on the domestic monetary policies of the countries between which they take place, more precisely, on the relationships between their respective domestic policies.

If the aim is to prevent or reduce undesirable movements of funds or to reverse certain movements, the interested governments will have to move far in the direction of concerting their policies in a manner that will adjust them to each other as much as possible. And since for every country monetary policy is a tool of economic management, no government can allow itself to alter its monetary policy in response to considerations of an international order unless it can obtain the results it considers desirable on the domestic scene by other means. The required coordination of monetary policies among the countries concerned is such that it affects the whole of their economic strategy.

It is less obvious, but no less true, that long-term capital movements can create a real problem only for the payments balances of the industrial countries. Developing countries do not export long-term capital. They import capital, of course, but the effect of these movements is generally quickly offset by purchases of equipment abroad that the capital imports enable them to finance. The upshot is that the balance of payments is not greatly affected. The balances of payments of the industrial countries, on the other hand, may be disturbed in two ways. It may happen that an industrial country makes investments in or loans to other industrial countries that lead to a deficit in its balance of payments and surpluses in theirs. It may also happen that one industrial country exports long-term capital to developing countries which, in disposing of the proceeds, make an abnormally large proportion of their purchases in other industrial countries. In this case also an imbalance would develop that could be charged to long-term capital movements. And it is clear that any such pattern would emerge mainly between countries having capital markets, that is, the eleven countries listed above. In this case as well, a special degree of cooperation among the countries with capital markets is to be recommended as a means of controlling such disequilibria, preventing them if possible, otherwise offsetting them or financing them.

Thus whether it is a question of short-term or long-term

capital movements, the very nature of things requires a few
countries to organize among themselves a special kind of collaboration and to provide supplementary financial facilities to
each other. These are the countries that have either a money
market or a capital market, and in most cases both, and that
deserve to be called "financial market countries."

The "financial market countries" are not the only ones with
special problems the solution of which is essential to the functioning of the international monetary system. The developing
countries also have special problems of their own.
While the developing countries are familiar with temporary
balance of payments crises arising from accidental circumstances that are amenable to the same sorts of remedies applied elsewhere, their monetary situation is affected in addition
by phenomena peculiar to themselves. These countries have a
continuing need for imports, particularly imports of capital
equipment, which they could only pay for from their own resources by reducing consumption to intolerable levels. To this
basic phenomenon, which is inherent in their status of developing countries, is added another, not so inherent, which burdens
their balances of payments: increases in the prices of manu-
factured products exported by the industrial countries are not
always accompanied, or often accompanied only after a delay,
by corresponding increases in the prices of the goods exported
by developing countries, which means that those countries face
an added difficulty in balancing their external accounts.
This chronic disequilibrium cannot logically be financed by
short- or medium-term credits. The developing countries need
long-term credits and investment from outside. Indeed, they
need credit at very long term and a low rate of interest. They
also need nonreimbursable assistance in the form of grants.
Finally, they need protection against an abnormal deterioration
in the relation between the prices of the industrial products
they import and the prices of the raw materials they export.
Coping with all these needs demands special measures.
Such measures, by their very nature, cannot be monetary.

But they have monetary implications. For in the absence of a
program of financial and economic cooperation for the benefit
of the developing countries, it is vain to expect that they can
establish equilibrium in their balances of payments and maintain acceptable parities or exchange systems. Solutions for the
special problems of these countries are therefore an indispensable element in any international monetary order.

The upshot is that to have an international monetary system
that functions adequately, three categories of problems must
be resolved: those common to all countries, those peculiar to
developing countries, and those peculiar to the financial market
countries.

It is the essential objective of the International Monetary
Fund to assure or facilitate the resolution of the problems
common to all countries: the evolution of the matrix of exchange rates, financing fluctuations in balances of payments
on current account, cooperation on the world scale, or nearly
so, with a view to maintaining freedom for current payments
and to maintaining a monetary climate that permits the growth
of international trade and financial relations.

The special problems of the developing nations are in no
sense of a monetary nature. Those of the financial market
countries are of a monetary nature to the extent that they result from short-term capital movements between countries of
this group, but of a nonmonetary nature to the extent that they
are related to the need for a sufficient degree of equilibrium
in the capital accounts of the countries concerned. But whether
or not they are monetary in their nature, the two categories of
problems are so in the sense that no international monetary
order is possible if they are not resolved.[11]

This point of view is in no way contrary to that held by the
drafters of the Bretton Woods charter. As we have said, they

---

11. We should note that there are very few countries that do not fall into
one or the other of the two categories described above. The only "developed" countries, apart from the Communist countries, that are not strictly
speaking "financial market countries" are a few Nordic or Mediterranean
countries of Europe, Austria, South Africa, Australia, and New Zealand.

were conscious of the need to superimpose on the Monetary
Fund another institution to deal with long-term capital. In creating the World Bank they did not assign to it only the task of
meeting the needs of the developing countries.

They had some illusions about the role the Bank could play
in covering the capital requirements of the industrial countries
impoverished by the war. They did not foresee the magnitude
that movements of short- and long-term capital between industrial countries would assume. They can hardly be criticized
for that. But they were aware that international credit operations beyond the scope of the World Bank and the Fund would
become necessary. They thought it would be premature to make
proposals on these matters, and they had confidence in the future. It is not their fault that the future only partly responded
to their aspirations. In any case, it is faithful to their trust to
endeavor today to establish what remains to be accomplished
in the way of cooperation among the financial market countries.

Why is it that during the twenty-five years that the charter
was in effect, what was achieved in this respect was inadequate
and fragile? Why was such obvious need not really recognized?
Why did the countries concerned tend to restrict their cooperation to discussions and resist admitting that cooperation necessarily implied reciprocal support? The responsibilities are
numerous.

The principal responsibility is that of the United States. Having undertaken certain commitments by its adherence to the
Bretton Woods agreements — even those circumscribed by Congress — the United States was averse to anything that might involve it in additional obligations, in particular any obligations
to contribute to covering an eventual capital deficit of European
or other foreign countries. On the other hand, the Americans
felt at ease in the Fund, which was installed in Washington, organized on American lines, and in which they had every reason
to believe that they could generally make their views prevail.
They could not have the same assurance of this in more restricted circles consisting only of industrial countries.

The International Monetary Tangle

This is why they have always been very careful to participate only cautiously in the activities of agencies for monetary cooperation other than the Fund. We have noted that they were only observers in the OEEC and the Management Committee of the EPU; that when they joined the OECD, they refused to take part in any monetary aspects of the work of the Organization; that while they found it useful to frequent Basel, they abstained from occupying their seats on the Board of the BIS; that they wanted the Group of Ten to be a sort of emanation — actually of an equivocal character — of the IMF; and that the arrangements for the "gold pool" remained informal.

Wanting to limit their gold losses and to cover as much as possible of their balance of payments deficit by other means, they sought, as was only natural, to do so by methods that safeguarded their freedom of action. In this they largely succeeded, thanks to the mechanics of the gold exchange standard, supplemented by a series of bilateral arrangements. When the Group of Ten envisaged the creation within the Group of a new reserve instrument of a collective character, and when in 1965 the Americans had arrived at the conclusion that this move could help them to finance their deficit if it was done in a manner that conformed to their views, they undertook — successfully — to get the discussion of the project moved into the sphere of the Fund, so that, with the aid of the developing countries, they could overcome the resistance they ran into on the part of the Europeans in the Group of Ten. Finally they managed, by and large, to cut down the importance of the Ten, to the profit of the almost worldwide Group of Twenty.

It would be unjust to infer from the above remarks that the men who have represented the United States since the war in the various organs of monetary collaboration among the financial market countries (OEEC, OECD, BIS, Group of Ten) have not been loyal and sincerely cooperative partners. They have almost always been that; the more so as most of them were convinced of the usefulness of such collaboration. But their good will was held in check by a reticence rooted in political circles and in the Congress.

Methods of International Monetary Cooperation

It would be no less unjust to blame only the United States for the fact that the collaboration we are discussing did not develop as it should have. In fact, nearly all parties concerned share some of the responsibility.

The staff of the Monetary Fund has always taken a poor view of anything done outside the Fund, and this tendency has grown stronger over the years. International organizations automatically assume that they are ends in themselves; they try to enlarge their attributions and push for a monopoly. The Managing Directors themselves have not been affected by this syndrome. Per Jacobsson on several occasions emphasized that there should be centers for monetary cooperation other than the Fund.

The third world has never wanted to concede that it was in conformity with its interests, properly understood, for the financial market countries to settle among themselves, in harmony with Fund objectives, the difficulties that concern only their relations with each other. They have never accepted the notion that the existence of those specific difficulties is no more abnormal than the existence of difficulties peculiar to the third world, and that the Fund is in no better position to deal with the first of these than with the second. The third world has always behaved as if monetary discussions among the industrial countries would be bound to end up being detrimental to their interests. They have always insisted on being included. They have always sought to convert their votes into cash, to gain additional advantages, and to try indirectly in this fashion to make up for the inadequacy of the aid furnished by the developed countries.

And finally, Western Europe, which one might think would have an interest in fighting for cooperation at the level of the Eleven, has on the whole put up a poor defense. The British position has always been wobbly. The British never seem to have abandoned the hope that the Fund would evolve toward the Keynesian pattern and thus enable them to find there a solution to part of their problems. They also seem to have hung on for a long time to the notion that the only viable monetary grouping outside the Fund was that of the two great reserve currencies. As for the continental Europeans, while they played an important

role in what was done in the early 1960s in the way of cooperation among the Eleven, after 1965 they were disunited as to
their conceptions of the problems and weakened, insofar as any
action was concerned, by the discords within the group.

The post-1971 situation provides a new setting for the problem. It has not caused it to disappear — far from it. It has not
done away with the vast movements of funds between the financial market countries. It has brought in an additional reason
for cooperation among those countries, namely, the need for
common action designed to control the floating of their currencies.

If the necessity for a real monetary cooperation among the
financial market countries could be recognized by the countries
or groups of countries concerned (the United States, Canada, the
European Economic Community, Switzerland, Sweden, and Japan), there would be no need for new institutions to make it effective. Above all, such cooperation requires a state of mind
and a will. It is a matter of the nations involved agreeing at
last to deal with the problems arising from actual or potential
movements of long- and short-term capital between them. Such
a design must include, on the one hand, concerted policies in
certain areas (interest rates, controls on national money and
capital markets and, in exceptional circumstances, on imports
and exports of capital) and, on the other hand, mutual financial
support designed to cover deficits as far as may be deemed appropriate and to avoid undesirable exchange rate movements.
The concerting of policies requires no new machinery. The
policies of the central banks are the concern of the Bank for
International Settlements, and within its framework these matters could easily be dealt with. As for government policies, the
OECD comes naturally to mind, since all the countries concerned are members; the fact that some other countries are
also members of the OECD would be no obstacle, judging by the
experience in Group No. 3 of the Economic Policy Committee.
It goes without saying that the governments involved could

94

choose some other meeting place for the purpose of concerting their policies if they so desired.

No new international mechanism is required for granting short- or long-term credits. The central banks, under the aegis of the BIS, have long been equipped with all necessary facilities for granting short-term credits. As for long-term credits, it is up to the countries that extend them to equip themselves to do so. When long-term American assistance was required in the immediate postwar period, the United States knew how to use, or invent, adequate machinery. If one day long-term credits from Europe and Japan are required to reduce the vulnerability of the dollar, it will be up to the countries concerned, in agreement among themselves and with the Americans, to put themselves in a position to lend the necessary amounts. Various formulas could, by the way, be used at the same time.

One can conceive of all sorts of modalities for activating this cooperation. But there is one point on which there should be no misunderstanding.

It is indispensable that the Monetary Fund and its members other than the financial market countries should be assured that what takes place among the financial market countries — which is one of the conditions for the proper functioning of the Fund itself — is consistent with the objectives of the Fund and in harmony with its activities. The first idea that comes to mind is that a good means of arriving at this result would be to activate this special cooperation in the form of a special section of the Fund — a sort of small club within the big club. But it is generally impossible in an international organization to have a circuit of discussions and operations open only to certain members and from which others are excluded without giving rise to psychological difficulties and tensions. It is almost inevitable that after a while the restricted club will become open to many members and finally to all. But the problems that the financial market countries need to resolve must be dealt with among themselves and cannot be adequately dealt with in a larger forum. The only satisfactory method, therefore, is to make the cooperation among the Eleven juridically independent from the Monetary Fund, while having the Managing Director of the Fund associated with all such activities, so as to insure that these always serve the objectives of the Fund and are never inimical to them. This is the method that was followed in the OEEC and the European Payments Union and which is still followed in Group No. 3 of the OECD. In both cases it has proved satisfactory. By contrast, what took place in the Group of Ten concerning the creation of a new reserve instrument well illustrates the dangers of a "little club within the big club" and also the demagogic maneuvers to which this leads. Either cooperation among the Eleven will work outside the Fund — albeit in liaison with it — or it will not work at all.

As for the World Bank, no one would dispute that either directly or through its affiliates it has performed an admirable job for the benefit of the developing countries. Nor is anyone likely to deny that the assistance rendered by the industrial countries to the developing countries has remained, qualitatively and quantitatively, inferior to what it ought to be. This immense topic is not within the scope of the present essay. It is only for us to repeat that even if the problem of aid is not in itself a monetary problem, it is so indirectly, to the extent that adequate aid for the developing countries is one of the preconditions of an international monetary order.

CHAPTER VIII

International Liquidity

Dollar Reserves

From around 1960 to 1971 it was not only the balance of payments deficit of the United States that caused trouble; it was,
perhaps even more, the technique used to finance the deficit.
The existence and the persistence of a large American deficit
constituted an important phenomenon and a cause for concern,
but should not have disorganized international payments as it
did. The United States owned foreign assets far in excess of its
liabilities to foreigners. These assets grew between 1958 and
1971, principally in the form of direct investments but also in
the form of short-term assets, to an extent that must have come
very close to equaling the cumulative total of all the deficits incurred during the period. The United States was a good credit
risk, and it would have been natural for its partners to have lent it
yearly — in a proper mix of long- and medium-term credits —
the resources required to finance the deficit until equilibrium
was restored. The ill effects of the accumulation of an enormous mass of dollars by the central banks could have been
avoided.

The Americans were the ones mainly responsible for this
situation. Never wanting to be in the position of having to seek

97

assistance either from the Fund or from other countries, they preferred the method of the gold exchange standard, which permitted them to go into debt without having to borrow and to do so in the form of obligations denominated in their own currency. But the other financial market countries were likewise at fault. They all behaved as if the Americans could finance themselves only by remitting gold or by recourse to the gold exchange standard. A few countries demanded full gold settlement, at least on some occasions; the others affected to consider dollars as the equivalent of gold. They should all, jointly, have offered the Americans credits.

They should have been the more ready to do this since in the immediate postwar period, when the United States was in surplus, it was American loans and grants that enabled the rest of the world to finance its disequilibrium. After 1958 many of the countries that had thus incurred long-term debts to the United States found it natural to prepay some of them. They should have considered it no less natural to lend to the United States. The continental European countries should have found it even more natural for the following reason. If the United States had not had the generosity to provide a large part of Marshall Plan aid in the form of grants, and if, as would then have been the case, their debts had been much larger, they would almost certainly have made prepayments on a much larger scale than they did.

There should have been American drawings on the Monetary Fund, at least to the extent that the balance of payments on current account was in deficit. Such drawings would have had the great psychological and political advantage of showing that the United States did not always escape completely from the application of the Bretton Woods charter. But in the main the credits should have been furnished by the members of the Group of Ten. It would not have been impossible to find in those countries the countervalue of around $3 billion a year, on the average, either as government loans or as public issues. And mobilizing those resources would have damped down the inflationary effects of the balance of payments surpluses.

International Liquidity

If such had been the policy of the Eleven (including the United States) many evils would have been avoided. When the devaluation of the dollar became necessary, it could have been carried out in an altogether different climate.

Looking now at what has happened since 1971 under the regime of floating, we must again assert that there was a lack of symmetry between the status of the dollar and that of the other principal currencies, with the inconveniences to which this gave rise.

The other countries held gold and dollars. If they needed ammunition to defend the value of their currencies on the market, they could, at least theoretically, make use of their gold either by selling it or using it for collateral. Above all, they could call on their dollar reserves without any difficulty. In the United States, by contrast, everything went on just as if they had no gold, since they no longer recognized any monetary role for the metal and seemed to regard their stocks of gold as a sort of inalienable war chest. As their policy was not to apply the practices of the gold exchange standard vis-à-vis other currencies that they had always encouraged their partners to practice vis-à-vis the dollar, they had very small amounts of foreign exchange balances.

The countries of Western Europe consider it entirely normal to borrow foreign currencies in case of need. They do it either by drawing on the Monetary Fund, by "swap" agreements between their central banks, or by negotiating loans in foreign currencies with other governments or on the international market. The United States, after having repudiated the "swap" method in principle in 1971, came back to using "swaps" between central banks; but they did it only for amounts which bear no relation to the volume of speculative movements of liquid assets that may need to be neutralized. With this exception the United States rejects the idea of foreign borrowings involving negotiations with lenders and an exchange risk. It continues to accept only the formula of foreign deposits or investments in dollars, more or less stimulated by interest rates.

The International Monetary Tangle

The United States having condemned itself to deploy only a small armament to defend its currency on the market, when the dollar has needed support, the principal effective means has been whatever purchases of dollars the central banks of other countries were disposed to make. But the initiative for such purchases does not rest with the United States — except to the extent that it can exert pressure on its partners. It has always been uncertain how far central banks would go in accumulating dollars, particularly considering the exchange risk to which they expose themselves. The United States, unlike other countries which incur debts, has the privilege of permitting its currency to depreciate without augmenting its foreign debt in terms of its national currency — except to the extent that it has utilized "swaps." These peculiar circumstances explain, at least in part, why on several occasions speculators have been able to attack the dollar in an irrational manner with wholly abnormal success.

All evidence suggests that the situation would have been both healthier and more balanced if the United States had done as its partners did and taken responsibility for the protection of its own currency. This would not have committed the United States to defend a fixed rate. But whatever exchange rate policy they might have chosen, it could have been carried out more effectively.

Precisely what techniques should have been used? The American authorities could have used "swap" agreements more systematically and for much larger amounts; they could have reactivated the technique of "Roosa bonds," which were used successfully during the 1960s and which made it possible to borrow from foreign central banks in the currency of the respective banks. They could have arranged facilities with other members of the Group of Ten or of the OECD. Whatever method was employed, it would have given confidence to the market, increased the risks run by speculators, and reinforced the chances for a durable stability of the dollar.

Let us again forget about events and reflect on the conditions

100

that monetary reserves must fulfill in order to perform their role properly.

If we abstract from reserves in gold (or, after they were created, Special Drawing Rights), the reserves of the various countries consist of credits they grant to each other. There are creditor countries whose net reserves are positive and debtor countries whose net reserves are negative. When a country in this second category[12] finds itself in difficulty (balance of payments deficit, exchange rate threatened), it normally needs supplementary credits from its partners during the time required to correct the situation; the amount and term of these credits should be established according to rational criteria. It needs a fortiori to have credits previously extended to it left outstanding. But if the country has contracted its debt through the mechanism of the gold exchange standard, exactly the opposite happens. Because of the exchange risk, masses of credits extended previously are withdrawn just when they are most needed, even if the country concerned is a completely solvent debtor. That is exactly what happened to the United States in the period before August 1971. Because they feared — quite justifiably — an exchange loss, America's creditors strangled it.

In other words, an automatic contraction in international liquidity is brought about just when an expansion would be desirable. The reserves disappear into thin air precisely when they are most needed.

It is therefore a bad technique to allow the international indebtedness by means of which reserves are constituted to be denominated, in excessive amounts, in the currency of the debtor. At the very least, creditors should have the possibility, to whatever extent they desire, to exchange their holdings for other credit instruments that would not expose them to the same exchange risk.

We should add that if a devaluation takes place in a country

---

12. The principal country belonging to this category is obviously the United States, whose net negative reserves had risen by the end of 1975 to nearly $60 billion.

101

that had attracted too many foreign owned deposits, that country's partners suffer a loss that cannot fail to leave unhappy memories. Belgium has never forgotten what the prewar devaluation of sterling cost her, and since that time the National Bank of Belgium has held no sterling balances. The devaluation of the dollar since 1971 has resulted in a considerable gain for the United States: the value of its external debt has fallen in relation to the value of the foreign assets that it was enabled to acquire by incurring the debt.

We have already become acquainted with the issues surrounding the gold exchange standard in our inventory of "myths and oversimplifications." We arrived at the conclusion that it would amount to chasing illusions, and not be desirable, to seek to outlaw this technique. But it is now clearly confirmed that the technique is dangerous and must be used cautiously.

Apart from the oil-exporting countries, the developing countries have neither the means to accumulate large reserves for long periods, nor are they accustomed to do so. Resort to the gold exchange standard, as a matter of fact, can only reach dimensions that become perilous on the world scale insofar as it affects relations among the financial market countries. Strengthened cooperation among those countries should therefore suffice to settle any questions in an appropriate fashion. It is up to the Eleven to prevent the accumulation of dollars from reaching excessive levels. It is also up to them to activate alternative methods that would permit excess dollar balances to be exchanged for other credit instruments not subject to the same drawbacks.

Such a policy must remain flexible and pragmatic. It must be delineated in the light of actual circumstances. Nevertheless, we can readily perceive some general ideas by which such a policy might fruitfully be guided.

Given the volume of international movements of funds, the balances of payments between the financial market countries are liable to undergo sudden reverses, and the debtor or creditor balances can quickly reach enormous figures. It could

happen in the future, in the event of American surpluses, that
the reserves of some other countries would be wiped out and
that in order to avoid disruptions of trade, American credits
would become necessary (especially if the United States refused to buy gold). One might say that in such a situation the
United States should accumulate foreign exchange; this is not
a realistic suggestion. We are thus led by several paths to the
concept of reciprocal credits within the framework of the Group
of Ten.[13]

On the other hand, the reluctance of central banks to accumulate the amount of dollars that control of the market would
sometimes require is often due not only to the exchange risk
they thus incur but also, and perhaps even more, to their concern not to inflate the domestic money supply. It would therefore be advantageous if the new credit instruments envisaged
could be discounted by the central banks on their domestic markets in a manner that would soak up liquidity. Let us recall
that when France needed to correct its monetary position
shortly before World War II, it procured the necessary foreign
exchange by means of borrowings by the French Treasury on
the Swiss and Dutch markets. Any suggestion that the U. S.
Treasury could borrow on foreign markets to cover part of a
deficit in the Federal budget would be greeted by smiles. The
idea certainly has no chance of being adopted. But it would be
entirely rational.

Gold

We have tried to show that it is beside the point to seek, as
many have, to draw from the experience of the past two decades
arguments in favor of a demonetization of gold or a reduction
of its role. This being said, would it be right or not to suppress
(or reduce) the use of gold?

---

13. We have alluded above (p. 57) to the American inspired proposal,
adopted by the OECD in 1975, envisaging the organization of a system of
mutual support among the member countries to deal with the oil deficits.
The proposal seemed to be a step in what we regard as the right direction.

The International Monetary Tangle

In order to avoid misunderstanding, let us first distinguish between the two monetary functions that the precious metal has traditionally fulfilled: as a standard of value and as a means of making settlements between central banks (or, if one prefers, as a money of account and as a means of payment). The record is quite different depending on whether one considers the one or the other function.

It has always been difficult to enforce gold clauses included in various international loans. They generally impose an excessive burden on the debtors. Experience has led to a preference for exchange-rate-guarantee clauses, which offer sufficient protection to the creditor without unreasonably burdening the debtor. For the same reason the system of the IMF may be criticized for denominating in gold the reciprocal debts and credits resulting from the Fund's operations. In the same way one can examine critically the merits of defining the value of national currencies as a certain weight of gold. This practice has, of course, never been sacrosanct. It is quite possible to use standards of reference other than the metal.

While gold may not have much future as a standard of value, it is very inconvenient to have to give it up as a means of settlement and as a reserve instrument. It is certainly possible from a purely technical viewpoint to conceive of a situation in which central banks ceased to hold stocks of gold and stopped using it in interbank settlements. But any attempt to do this would run into great difficulties at the political level.

A country holding reserves in the form of gold is assured of being able to use it for payments anywhere and under any circumstances, even in the case of diplomatic tension and even in case of war. A country holding all its reserves in the form of dollars or in the form of a fiduciary currency represented by credit balances on the books of an institution located in Washington may be exposed to various risks if certain circumstances arise: the risk that some countries will not accept payment in the fiduciary money as a discharge of debt; the risk that the U. S. government might place controls on transactions on the books of American banks or on those of the Washington institution.

104

Experience has shown that the solemn agreements guaranteeing the privileges of international institutions resist poorly the pressures of public opinion and national parliaments in wartime. Countries holding their reserves in this form may find themselves cut off from some parts of the world. They place themselves, in fact, in fee to the United States.

One section of the planet, that occupied by the Communist nations, has chosen gold. This choice has no doubt been made, among other reasons, for political considerations of the sort just referred to. If one wants to be able in all circumstances to make payments to those countries, notably commercial payments, it must be possible to make them in gold. If one wants to be able to receive payments from them, notably in settlement of an export surplus, it must be possible to accept gold from them and to be able to take the gold into the accounts at a price that does not clearly undervalue it. All the more reasons why gold reserves valued on the basis of a realistic price are useful. Another point to be made is that the International Monetary Fund was designed to be universal in scope, and it was foreseen at the beginning that the Communist countries would join; their adherence, made impossible for the time being by the cold war, remains desirable. The demonetization of gold and the failure to revalue it would make such a development more difficult, if not impossible.

The advantages of a recourse to gold are, moreover, not uniquely political. The metal's detractors often assert that the world would risk foundering in deflation because the stock of monetary gold does not necessarily grow with the regularity and at the pace that would be desirable. This objection applies to a regime in which the metal was the only international means of payment to the exclusion of any credit component. Such a pure gold standard regime has probably never existed. In any case, it is not such a regime that has existed since World War II, since deficit countries have benefited from multiple facilities — in the first place, the right to draw on the Monetary Fund. A judiciously conceived system of international payments should provide resources in addition to gold — resources endowed with sufficient elasticity. But it should impose on deficit countries (at least as concerns industrial countries) a parallelism in the utilization of their metallic reserves and their other resources in order to reestablish, through the indirect effects of gold losses, a certain discipline. This is a supplementary argument in favor of the metal. Even if the United States refused to accept such discipline, other countries could decide by common accord to preserve it in relations among themselves (for example, if there were an agreement for the mutual granting of credits among the members of the European Economic Community).

Conscious of the difficulties posed by the adoption of a new official price for the metal, some excellent minds have asked whether an acceptable compromise solution might not be as follows: central banks would continue to hold gold reserves and use the metal in settlements with each other, but they would abstain from trying to stabilize the market price.

This solution might be a lesser evil. In itself there is little to be said for it. It would be highly inconvenient for central banks to buy, sell, and account for gold on the basis of a fluctuating price. On the other hand, the fluctuations on the free gold market, which is normally a very narrow market, are subject to influences that ought not to affect the value of the metallic reserves of central banks. The truth is that the moment a high enough new official price of gold was established, the central banks should have no difficulty getting the market to sanction it. It is easily forgotten that gold is in a unique position among commodities in that the stocks of metal in the vaults of central banks amount to about forty times the quantity exchanged annually between producers and users. On the other hand, production is normally greater than the nonmonetary demand. This explains why, despite the decline of confidence in the dollar, a gold price that was obviously too low could be respected by the market up to 1966 without the "gold pool" having to lose metal. It could scarcely be justified on the part of the central banks not to stabilize the market at the level of an

International Liquidity

official price regarded as realistic.
Let us not forget that, in some countries at least, the price
at which gold is traded on the free market has a psychological
importance and that stability of that price is an element of confidence both in the national currency and in the international
monetary system. Rational or not, this reflex is a reality that
must be taken into account. It constitutes one more argument
for establishing a new official gold price that would be respected by the market.

Special Drawing Rights

Excessive reliance on the gold exchange standard is dangerous. Recourse to gold meets objections. There is a great temptation to seek a solution in a fiduciary instrument of a multinational character that would gradually become the principal
component of reserves. We have noted that since 1971 the international community has endeavored to reach an agreement
to put this idea into effect and that, for the time being, it has
given up the attempt. The exceptional increase in reserves in
the form of dollars furnished the pretext. In fact, the negotiations were making little progress.
The idea is often put forward that individual countries manu-
facture monetary instruments which constitute legal tender in
their territories and that, on the whole, this leads to no very
dramatic consequences. But this fabrication of money is the
act of central banks, which, however much their autonomy is
restricted today, do have the authority vis-à-vis governments
that inheres in the necessity to show on the asset side of their
balance sheets some respectable counterpart. Moreover, the
undue creation of fiduciary instruments within a country is subject to a double sanction: that of people who hold cash and can
convert it into real assets, and that of the balance of payments,
which prevents any one country from indulging in a rate of inflation greater than that of the international community in general without suffering the consequences. On the contrary, the

107

The International Monetary Tangle

creation of international reserve instruments would be done by
the collectivity of the member governments of the Monetary
Fund. To picture a comparable mechanism on the national
scale, you have to imagine the volume of money creation as
being the object of a decision by the parliament. You must
imagine that there was only one country in the world and that
it would thus be able to ignore balance of payments problems.
Finally, you must suppose that in such a country there was no
possibility of fleeing from the currency in favor of other assets. Who can doubt that in this sort of situation there would
be a considerable risk of excessive money creation?

The experience with Special Drawing Rights has not been
very reassuring in this respect. When the instrument was under study, it was understood that it would only be used in the
event of the danger of a shortage of reserve instruments following upon an improvement in the American balance of payments.
But under U.S. pressure it was decided to create $9 billion of
SDRs when there was clearly already too much international
liquidity. On the other hand, the developing countries sought to
have part of the allocations of SDRs take the form of additional
aid, which was in direct contradiction to the solemnly proclaimed objective of the operation — to provide supplementary
resources to central banks. During the abortive negotiations
after 1971, the third world countries understandably renewed
their demand that future creations of SDRs should be used to
provide at least a partial solution to the aid problem.

If, therefore, as is quite possible, circumstances lead the
members of the Fund to decide again one day to issue fiduciary
money, there should be no illusions about the inflationary risks
that the operation will entail.

The Eurocurrency Market

The Eurodollar market (or rather, the Eurocurrency market,
since currencies other than the dollar, mainly the mark, now
play a not insignificant role), because of the functions it performs

and the dimensions it has attained, has become one of the components of the international monetary system. This banking network extends to several continents and is capable of rendering services that no national banking system can offer.

The dangers involved are well known. Free from control by the national monetary authorities, banks operating in Eurocurrencies run the risk of not adjusting the terms of their loans to those of their borrowings, in other words, to finance medium-term credits on the basis of short-term resources. They risk making too adventurous loans, particularly being too free with their facilities for the benefit of deficit countries, thus allowing them to escape from the discipline that other lenders would impose (governments or the IMF).

The banks dealing in Eurocurrencies seem, on the whole, to be aware of these dangers. Some imprudent actions led to accidents during the recession of 1974 and served as a warning. The situation is probably healthier today than it was two years ago. The amount of credit extended to some debtor countries remains, however, a matter of concern. While the monetary authorities of the various countries, after losing a lot of time, seem to have arrived at a relatively correct view of the dimensions of the market and the main lines of its activity with the aid of the BIS, it does not appear that they have agreed among themselves to exercise a control on the banks engaged in those activities anything like what applies in each country to banking transactions in the national currency. The domestic monetary policy of each country is thus subject to the risk of being frustrated. And one wonders whether certain central banks of the Group of Ten are not continuing, directly or indirectly, to invest some of their exchange reserves in a market that to some extent presents a challenge to their national regulations. But having said this, it is not in the domain of the Eurocurrency market that the principal problems of today's international monetary regime are to be found.

CHAPTER IX

The Ambiguities of the American Position

The American position on international monetary issues is complex and often disconcerting. It is the resultant of two forces. One is the instinctive tendency that pushes the United States toward monetary "egocentrism." The other force is the feeling, prevailing in various circles, that to go too far in that direction would be contrary to the fundamental objectives of U. S. foreign policy.

In order to understand the first tendency, it may be best to follow its logic and state in its extreme form the doctrine to which it leads. That doctrine is approximately the following:

The United States must be able to manage its own affairs as it thinks best. It must be able to determine in complete independence its fiscal policy, its full-employment policy, its growth policy. The American nation needs no external pressure to make it keep watch to assure that its economy and its dollar remain healthy. Foreign trade, moreover, constitutes a relatively small percentage of all economic activities in the United States. It should not be given too much weight in general policy.

The United States should not be overly concerned about fluctuations in its balance of payments. Foreign countries have no reason to complain about accumulations of dollars that may result from such fluctuations. Furthermore, what could they do with their reserves that would be better than holding dollars? Apart from Britain, the other financial market countries have never sought to provide a haven for international liquid assets, the volume of which is excessive in relation to their absorptive capacities. As for Britain, it is no longer in shape to perform this function adequately, except in the form of operations in Eurodollars, with respect to which the London market in reality plays an auxiliary role to New York.

In addition, the U.S. authorities make an effort to place the American banks in a position to offer attractive returns on foreign-owned assets. This may lead to occasional conflicts with national policy on interest rates. But compromises are possible. The Eurodollar technique developed around 1960 is one means of reconciling a low return on domestic deposits with an attractive return on deposits collected abroad.

As long as gold played a monetary role and the dollar was convertible, foreign holders could be tempted to leave the dollar for gold, as General de Gaulle did with éclat around 1965. But gold convertibility was a deplorable survival from the past. The demonetization of the metal is essential. Today it seems to have been accomplished, and the dollar no longer has any rival.

Of course, the project of making out of the SDR a true international fiduciary currency issued by the Fund might be activated. But the SDR would not endanger the dollar. It goes without saying that the modalities of SDR creation and of their distribution would be established in agreement with the United States. The necessary arrangements could be made to insure that eventual conversions of dollars into SDRs could take place without leading to undesirable strains.

In fact, for the United States the very notion of a balance of payments makes no sense. Periodic publication of the outcome of foreign trade is necessary, because the country must be careful to maintain the positive trade balance that is indispensable. It must be able to live up to its foreign commitments for

security and international solidarity. It must also be able to
finance the traditional flow of its capital exports (especially in
the form of direct investments), which business circles would
never admit should be permanently restricted by controls.

But the publication of the results of what pretends to be a
balance of payments is harmful. It should be abandoned. International operations in dollars are so complex that all possible
formulas for presenting a balance are imperfect and hardly in-
telligible. Above all, the very concept of a U.S. balance of payments directs opinion and the markets toward unreal problems.

For analogous reasons, the Federal Reserve and the Treasury
do not need to hold foreign exchange reserves. The gold stock
ought to be placed in the same category as stockpiles of stra-
tegic materials. If in the course of its daily operations the Federal Reserve for technical reasons happens to buy and sell foreign exchange, any amounts that are held over should be regarded as working balances. American taxpayers should not
be asked to bear the risks of losses on foreign exchange.

Congress should keep a close eye on the "swap" arrangements that the New York Federal Reserve Bank negotiates with
foreign central banks. To the extent that these operations have
the effect of lending dollars to countries in deficit, they raise
no difficulty in principle (but they should not get too big). But
if they develop in another direction and lead to borrowing
abroad, this would mean that the United States was contracting
debts denominated in currencies other than its own — which is
not acceptable. These "swaps" must not go beyond what is required for carrying out a modest action of evening out daily
fluctuations in the market.

The "swaps" exemplify the dangers to which the administration and the Federal Reserve System (particularly the Federal
Reserve Bank of New York) are exposed by participating without due forethought in the work of institutions such as the OECD
or the Bank for International Settlements. American participation in such organizations should be limited to exchanges of
views and efforts to arrive at common policies. It should exclude anything that would entail financial obligations. In any

case, any such commitments could only be entered into with Congressional authorization.

The only organism for international monetary cooperation of which the United States recognizes that it is a full member is the Fund created at Bretton Woods. Even here it must be realized that insofar as the setting of exchange rates is concerned, the situation no longer allows the United States to accept vis-à-vis the Fund the same obligations that it accepted in 1944. At that time the stability of the relationship between gold and the dollar and the convertibility of the dollar appeared to be secure forever. The United States alienated none of its sovereignty in joining a system in which parities could be changed only with the approval of the Fund. In addition, Congress had taken all necessary precautions in ratifying the Articles of Agreement of the Fund. Today the fact is, as has been admitted since August 1971, that we live in a world that has profoundly changed. Convertibility of the dollar into gold has become impossible; it has been suspended; it will never be re-established.

Since the American authorities do not engage in operations in anything but dollars (with the single exception of the "swaps"), they cannot assume responsibility — at least no direct responsibility — for fluctuations that may take place in the value of the dollar in foreign markets. These fluctuations are an external event as far as the United States is concerned. It is up to other countries to decide to what extent, through sales or purchases, they wish to raise or lower the value of their currencies in relation to the American currency.

This does not mean that the United States is indifferent to what happens on foreign markets. It is concerned about avoiding the risk of competitive devaluations by certain countries. It can oppose such practices by using various means of pressure it has available, either in the framework of the Monetary Fund or at the bilateral level. It may, on occasion, wish to see an attack made on speculators when they are behaving in a manner that is detrimental to the dollar. Thus the Americans are led to take an interest in the policies of intervention engaged in

by other countries. They may also be inclined to try to influence such policies. But their own action as buyers or sellers
of exchange can only be very limited. The main instrument
they have available is the manipulation of their interest rates
to the extent that powerful domestic considerations leave them
free enough to do so.

When all is said and done, it must be accepted that there is
a generic difference between the dollar and other currencies.
The dollar is at once a national currency and the international
currency. The other kinds of money are mainly national currencies — one dare not say local currencies. The Eurodollar
phenomenon well epitomizes this reality. After all, what is the
significance of the Eurodollar? It is that in every country in
the world, parallel to the banking operations in the national
currency, there has developed a system of banking operations
in dollars. It consists in large part of credit transactions in
which the United States is not concerned, sometimes of transactions between borrowers and lenders in the same country.
Everything goes on as if each foreign country had two currencies — its own and the dollar.

We have carried to an extreme — perhaps almost to the extent of caricature — this description of the "egocentric" attitude. We hasten to say that in any such radical form it has been
advanced only by some intellectuals (notably economists of the
"benign neglect" school) and in some Congressional circles.
The administration does not seem to have adopted this view except for a short time after August 1971. The fact is that the responsible authorities have nearly always been conscious of the
contradiction that exists between this view and the general di-
plomacy and international economic policy of the United States.

The posture of "egocentrism" is more than merely egotis-
tical. It is a cynical attitude and, to a degree, combative. It is
not likely to provoke reprisals since the partners of the United
States are too much afraid of irritating the Americans. It seems,
nevertheless, to be one of the causes of the current confusion

114

in international monetary affairs, of the instability of exchange
rates, and of the disorder in the gold market. American policy
during the last few years has been a factor in the disintegration
of Western Europe.

The United States finds it natural when in deficit to be the
beneficiary of unconditional and unlimited credit. But when it
is in surplus, it has no obligation to extend credit and no mechanism for doing so (apart from the "swaps," which can only be
limited, short-term facilities). The United States expects its
partners to accumulate dollars without limit, but itself holds
no or almost no foreign currencies. When the value of the dollar is unquestioned, as it was at the end of World War II, they
arrange to have the world community adopt a system, indeed a
benign one, designed to subject devaluations to a form of control. But when, as in 1971, it is the dollar that is overvalued,
they have the system declared defunct and remove all brakes
on devaluations. These perceived facts are inevitably bitterly
resented.

Since World War II the United States has devoted enormous
efforts and considerable sums to encourage the reestablishment and the maintenance of order in Europe and, if it were
possible, the birth of a European unity. The Americans have
been pleased to find allies on the old continent that were not
mere satellites. At the same time, they have consistently followed a policy on the world scale to encourage the growth of
trade and the dismantling of tariff barriers. The Tokyo Round
of tariff negotiations, going on now, is one part of this program.
There is a clear incompatibility between all this constructive
action and the destructive effects to which the "egocentric" line
of conduct risks leading.

We have seen, in tracing the events on the international monetary scene from 1943 to 1976, that American policy has been
characterized by ambiguity, by apparent discontinuities, and by
often disconcerting changes. This is because it has had two
permanent components. In the face of the strong "egocentric"

115

current, the responsible authorities have had to tack even when they were fully conscious of the dangers involved.

What has been true for more than thirty years will in all probability remain true in the period ahead. The two forces will continue to clash, and any decisions will be compromises. The most one can hope for is that in the future more attention than has been the case during the past ten years will be paid to the fundamental foreign policy of the United States.

Final Remarks

Having passed in review the successive manifestations of international monetary cooperation since World War II, we have arrived at the conclusion that the best system for determining exchange rates should probably be based on principles analogous to those of Bretton Woods, but allowing for the possibility of a temporary recourse to floating exchange rates in exceptional circumstances. It does not seem to be a good idea to attempt to demonetize gold. We have suggested that it would be desirable to organize a renewed form of collaboration among the financial market countries, including the United States, involving reciprocal credits of a substantial size.

The new regime installed after August 1971 was born under the inspiration of very different ideas, notably, the idea that the formula of floating currencies is intrinsically superior. But this regime has evolved. The concept of free floating has never, in fact, been strictly applied. There has been a movement toward controlled floating, which in the end could become something not very different in practice from a system of fixed exchange rates.

Actually, there is more than one road by which to reach the essential objectives — freedom for transfers and a reasonable degree of exchange stability.

The International Monetary Tangle

On the eve of the 1939-45 war, a certain international monetary order had been established. It did not involve the creation
of a world institution. It rested on an understanding between
the American and British governments, expressed concretely
by the maintenance of a cross rate between the dollar and the
pound and on agreements that after 1936 brought into an association with that entente France (this was the Tripartite Agreement between France, Britain, and the United States), Belgium,
the Netherlands, and Switzerland. Parallel to the intergovern-
mental arrangements, the central banks of Western Europe and
Japan, as well as the American Federal Reserve System, coop-
erated in the framework of the Bank for International Settlements. The method seemed to be fully capable of leading to
the desired end.

From 1945 to 1971 the pillar of monetary collaboration among
nations was the Fund founded in 1944. This solution turned out
to be a good one, at least for about two decades.

Today, through the force of circumstances, an intermediate
formula seems to be gaining ground. The Fund would continue
to play an important role on the world scale, but the extent of
its supervision over the setting of exchange rates would be reduced. The system would also be based on collaboration among
the financial market countries, especially between the United
States and the Federal Republic of Germany. The relative stability between the mark and the dollar that should thus be assured could play the role of a keystone somewhat comparable
to that of the sterling-dollar cross rate of the prewar period.
There is no reason why such a formula could not lead to an acceptable modus vivendi. The question is to know under what
conditions it could do so. Our examination shows that there
are four such conditions.

The first concerns inflation. It is vain to hope for exchange
stability between countries whose currencies are depreciating
internally at markedly different rates. And when the rate of internal depreciation is abnormally high for most countries, there
is no chance that the rhythm of inflation can be kept equal for
any length of time in the various countries — even within an

economic grouping like the European Common Market. Adequate exchange stability can only be achieved among countries that have mastered inflation.

Inflation is one of the great problems of our time. It is not within the scope of this essay to deal with it as such. But we must state forcefully that unless inflation can be conquered, there can be no satisfactory international monetary regime.

The elimination of inflation is a national responsibility in each country. It is the job of each people to clean up before its own front door. But it is no less true that the international monetary mechanisms should not negate the efforts of governments in this domain and that they should, insofar as possible, support them. From this viewpoint there is reason to pay close attention to the Eurocurrency markets, which in several respects may contribute to inflation. Equally dangerous is the temptation some countries may feel to profit from the facility of floating exchange rates — along with the facility of having access to borrowing in the Eurocurrency market — by allowing themselves to slide too readily down the slope of monetary erosion. Considering the weakening of the power of the IMF, it must be largely within the framework of the group of financial market countries that action should be taken to prevent this sort of abuse. But this is possible only if this group becomes a reality.

Reinforcement of the collaboration among the financial market countries (or among the countries members of the OECD) is the second necessary condition for the present regime to attain its objectives. The existence of an enormous mass of liquid assets, which are only placed in the markets of the Eleven and which leave one of those markets only to move to another, creates problems within that group of countries that are sui generis and that necessitate a special degree of cooperation. This cooperation cannot be confined to a simple "concertation." It requires a network of very large mutual credits. The group of countries concerned must establish liaison with the Fund in order to satisfy the latter that nothing transpires among the Eleven contrary to the interests of the whole international community.

119

The International Monetary Tangle

Financial solidarity among the Eleven is even more indispensable today, when the policies of the oil-exporting countries accentuate the disparities in the situations of the industrial countries; those in which the increases in reserves of the oil-exporting countries are deposited are not those whose balances of trade are most severely affected by the rise in oil prices. It is therefore desirable — as the U.S. government wisely proposed in 1974 — that a mechanism of mutual support should be allowed to function as between the industrial countries belonging to the two groups.

The third condition relates to the developing countries with deficits — deficits that have generally been aggravated today by the rise in oil prices. It has been very useful for these countries, in recent years, to have received large credits from commercial banks in the industrial countries. But such credits can only provide a partial solution. The only sound formula for aid to these countries is grants or long-term, low-interest loans. And it goes without saying that the oil-exporting countries should provide a just share of the necessary assistance. Not to resolve the problems of the developing nations would be to leave in place a threat to the equilibrium of the international monetary and banking systems.

The fourth condition relates to the position of the United States. The exchange rate of the dollar needs to be better protected than at present against future speculative attacks, which are always possible. To this end the American authorities must consent to take responsibility for the defense of their currency on the foreign exchange market, as is done by the authorities of the other countries. Foreign central banks should be given the option of exchanging their dollar balances for other credit instruments that would not have the same disadvantages for them. To this end the American authorities should accept without reservation the notion that in some circumstances the United States should incur debts denominated in currencies other than the dollar. In other words, the United States should accept, along with a reinforced cooperation with the other financial market countries, a greater degree of symmetry — or

Final Remarks

at least less lack of symmetry — between the status of the dollar and that of other currencies.

The tendency that we have labeled "egocentric" pulls the United States in an opposite direction. The chances for a favorable evolution of international monetary relations depend, therefore, to a large extent on the response that the future will provide to the following question. Will the United States become sufficiently aware of the fact that its instinctive monetary "egocentrism" is in conflict with the fundamental objectives of its foreign policy and with its true interests?

About the Author

Guillaume Guindey was born in 1909 at Evreux, France. He graduated from the Ecole Normale Supérieure (philosophy) and Ecole Libre des Sciences Politiques, and entered the Inspectorate General of Finance in the French Ministry of Finance in 1932. He was responsible for international affairs in the Ministry of Finance from 1943 to 1953 (Algiers and Paris); was President, Societé des Mines de Cuivre de Mauritanie, 1953-58, Director General of the Bank for International Settlements (Basel), 1958-63, and President, Supervisory Board of Caisse Centrale de Cooperation Economique (Paris), 1965-72. M. Guindey took part in most major international financial negotiations from 1944 to 1965. While holding various positions in both French and foreign private business firms in recent years, he has written numerous articles on international monetary problems and the first edition of this book, Mythes et Réalités de la Crise Monétaire Internationale (Paris, 1973).

M. Guindey is also the author, among other works, of Théologie d'un Laïc (Paris, 1968) and Le Drame de la Pensée Dialectique: Hegel, Marx, Sartre (Paris, 1974).